Dear Daisy,

Thank you for always supporting my work and reading my books. I hope you enjoy this edition of Cul-de-sac Angels. Take care ♡

CUL-DE-SAC ANGELS

All the best,

Michelle Jarvis

CUL-DE-SAC ANGELS

MICHELLE GARCIA

Copyright © 2023, 2021 by Michelle Garcia

All rights reserved. No part of this book may be scanned, uploaded, reproduced, distributed, or transmitted in any form or by any means whatsoever without express permission from the author, except in the case of brief quotations embodied in critical articles and reviews. Thank you for supporting the author's rights.

Printed in the United States of America

First edition published 2021.

ISBN: 979-8-218-08580-3

Cover art by Matthew Glover
Interior media by Michelle Garcia

For more information, visit www.michellegarciawrites.com.

*For my greatest teachers,
Mom and Dad*

CONTENTS

I **CREATION MYTH**	**1**
II **GHOST STORIES**	**29**
III **LOVE LETTERS**	**61**
IV **BOOK OF REVELATION**	**81**
V **WAR DIARY**	**105**
VI **SWAN SONGS**	**123**
Gratitude	145
Author Bio	148

"Heaven did not seem to be my home; and I broke my heart with weeping to come back to earth; and the angels were so angry that they flung me out into the middle of the heath on the top of Wuthering Heights; where I woke sobbing for joy."

— EMILY BRONTË, *WUTHERING HEIGHTS*

I

Creation Myth

Strange Paradise

I thirst for strawberry summers, my nine-year-old body
outstretched on the grassy slope of our front yard.
It is noon and I smell of community pool chlorine
and not nearly enough sunscreen. The world is good
and I am aware of this, shoulders burnt pink enough
to start a fire, sky so cloudless I imagine dipping my toes
into it, finding no bottom, and sinking into some strange
paradise. But I blink and there I am on my back again,
and the mailwoman has arrived with nothing important,
just grocery store coupons, a water bill, and a wave hello,
and I wave hello back, because I am nine summers young
and I believe in the kindness of cul-de-sac angels and that I,
freckled and peachy, play a part in a good, good world.

Bedroom Collection 1/2

I.

Chipped bubblegum walls, nail-sized hole in the ceiling
from the Christmas morning Dad hung a princess canopy
over the quilted twin bed and I, being just five earthly years,
nearly died of rejoicing. There's a snow globe collection
(*Kansas City, The Big Apple, some Canadian province
with a funny name*) hidden next to stacks of early 2000s
DVDs dusted over by 18 years of girlhood magic. From that
window I used to watch the tulip poplar rooted in our yard
blossom and shed like an honorable prostitute. I remember
when she finally succumbed to the kind of malignant cancer
ancient trees inherit and the bad men in trucks came to uproot
and dethrone her and kidnap my only friend away. That day
they left an abyss in the ground still so terribly unnatural that
even now our grass only grows deep green around it, as if forever
stunted by what unspeakable crime (*the breaking of my heart*)
had been committed there.

II.

                       I want to tell you another story
about that window and the foreign flavors it offered me. The
awkward stage of my 13th spring I perched there with Dad's
pocket-sized binoculars to observe, with my freckled girl friend,

the boy with the floppy brown almost-mullet playing Shirts
versus Skins on the sloping field by the middle school we attended.
We'd just watch, illiterate in the male species, giggling through
tight braces like schoolgirls because that's exactly what we were.
Three years later a boy with another name stood beneath the window
as valiant and hormonal as Shakespeare's Romeo and "promposed"
to me with pink roses in his hand by reading poetry from computer
paper written in Crayola marker. I said yes yes yes (*and ran like mad
downstairs to thank him for letting me play his blushing Juliet*).

III.

In that room I grew to be small and jealous and in love
with worlds apart from it. That place is now a portal
to a dimension where I was once innocent enough to believe
in simple things: bedtime prayers, the oak desk permanently
stained with yellow acrylic paint, dog-eared books
(*Sylvia Plath's Ariel, my adolescent journals, The Velveteen Rabbit,
The Nutcracker Ballet, an unread copy of Anna Karenina*)
tucked in secret nooks, Polaroids of now-strangers ruined
by terrible exposure, names of pop star crushes I scrawled
on the wall behind my mattress. Nothing vaguely unholy
ever happened there, in that suburban dollhouse of a room
where the inimitable smells of summer (*neighbor's barbecue,
bug spray, sidewalk chalk, chlorine and backyard sprinkler*)
wafted in, and I took it all in, inhaled every atom of it,
because I was young and because there was nothing better to do
and no one better to be.

As Kids

We were smart. Cul-de-sac geniuses
in hand-me-down Bermuda shorts.
My cousins and I, we were raised by
the Backstreet Boys on the boombox,
Kodak disposables, scraped knees.
I am nostalgic now, for that textbook
Americana, 25-cent lemonade stands
and yard sales where we'd bid farewell to
outgrown tricycles and pink dollhouses.

We could braid, too. French and Dutch
and other styles we'd invent on the fine,
blonde hair of our American Girl dolls.
I remember wanting hair like that—
gold like the movie stars' on the posters
Scotch-taped to my bubblegum walls.

Reduced to mythology now, practically
fiction, the only leftovers still remaining
are the lives we abandoned under plastic
sleeves in the albums we only flip through
when we come home for Christmas break.

We were unmanufactured. Scruffy, wild,
grass-stained and privileged. Sidewalk

rulers, gods and monsters of blanket forts
and summer sprinklers and shared family.

Sometimes I close my eyes and it's 2004
and we're in the hammock, just me and my
cousins, and we're a sticky heap of August,
banana-scented sunscreen, and tenderness.

It Is August 28, 2004

And I'm a monster with a milk mustache
stirring Froot Loops to make the colors run.

Today is a good day.

Today I will arrange my plastic figurines
in a summoning circle. Ronald McDonald,
Snow White, Winnie-the-Pooh, Spider-Man.
I like it when my best friends hold hands.

I also like summer.

Summer means haircuts by Mom in the kitchen,
streamers and training wheels and even a bell
that Dad installed for me to call the neighbor's
cats. There is no need to dream if I live in one.

I have everything.

I am almost five and I am scared of fireworks
and the big dogs down the street and one day
I want to be an astronaut but won't actually
go to space because space is big for someone
small like me. But enough about one day,
because today I will just dance in the sprinkler.

I know everything there is to know
about everything worth knowing.

Like how you shouldn't open your eyes
in the public pool or they will sting bad.
And how crayons don't taste the way
they look. And how sometimes people
fall asleep and we cry about it and when
you hold their hand they don't hold back.

I don't like it.

But I like that today is the last Saturday of summer
and I'm not in space. I'm four. I'm home.

And I am so proud to be loved like this.

Luddite

Before there were screens we were magic.
Before we started crossing streets with faces
glued to glass, before we began seeking out
love in Google searches, *14,580,000,000
results (0.68 seconds) but never one exact
enough to capture the whole of it.* I miss
being part of a world that loved me back,
a living piece of its anatomy, apart from
this instantaneous, delirious, nauseating
madness. I remember when I was young,
using my hands. Kneading bread with
bare palms, dough collapsing under my
weight, holy labor. And later, plucking
tomatoes from the vine, beads of sweat
collecting at the hairline, nothing to
preserve the moment but that feeling
of worthiness, that my shoulders, *mine,
my own,* had been chosen by the sun
to be kissed like that. I can't remember
the last time my hands moved that
gently, assembling and dismantling
the invisible frame of reality. Know this.

I once touched the bones of this world.
I scattered fingerprints on real things.

I Was Five and I Knew

I knew everything there is to know
by the time I turned five. Like *rain*—

it is for swaddling your bones in quilts
and listening, motionless,
nothing else,
just listening.

If you do so close enough, it sounds a lot
like how the idea of God makes some people
believe in things unseen. I knew then
that I was made for blind faith.

The sky is an open book. It will whisper
its origin stories and saturate your shoulders
with its wisdom if you lean into it,
if you look up.

I was five and I knew
that nothing else could ever teach me more.

Where Do Poems Come From?

I can't speak for yours,

but mine—

they fall from the apple trees of memory:

[lunchbox love letters my mother would pack
under kindergarten grilled cheese sandwiches]

[certain smells, like fresh oregano and Old Spice
deodorant and the last day of summer in Virginia]

[the curvature of my first love's cheek, too familiar]

[my heart glowing under tender peacoat buttons
all winter, as if I had swallowed a lamp for you]

[the worst pain I've ever felt]

Oh,

how they thud against unforgiving earth,

while I bend down to juice what is left

of each bruised

[and beautiful]

little world.

Montage

You know, the smell after rain in the suburbs
is perfect for dancing barefoot in the backyard.

This is an indisputable fact of my universe—
a truth I know like the back of my own hand,
my first language, a special kind of mother tongue.

I have memorized that, every April without fail,
dandelions populate the cracks in the sidewalk
leading to our front door. How I used to pick them,
filling my fists with that tug and pull, all of that bright
yellow weed overflowing my mother's vases,
bookmarking the pages of half-finished chapters,
sunshine spilling over everywhere I dared to put it.

You know, things grow back there,
in that place (less place, more memory now)
I call home, where a small child still runs,
excavating, uprooting, part-time archaeologist
and full-time preserver of beauty.

It's true. Things really grow back there.
Like dandelions, thunderstorms,
and backyard waltzes with first loves long gone.

Girls do, too—ones like me,
with small hands and big dreams,
always reaching for something to pull from the earth.

How Wild and Limitless

Pathetically depleted, I wallow in my flesh and dream
of a particular kind of freedom. The painless, childish
sort, like when you're seven and your whole life orbits
around the geometric dome at your elementary school
playground and trading juice boxes for scented erasers.
Holding twenty years in your hands is a great ordeal,
heavier than expected, unlike the gala apples you'd pack
for field trips and forget in the tall grass for picnic ants
to call their own. At seven you don't think much about
pain or the body or what is written in the stars for you.
You just know you like to run, and then you skin your
knee and train yourself to avoid that particular sidewalk
crack forever after, and the only stars you care about
are the ones that twinkle extra hard on your birthday,
and the ones on movie screens, and the ones in your eyes
when you think about how wild and limitless the world
is, the entire sphere inhaling and exhaling just for you.

Ode to Strange Fixations

At ten, it was eating, not picking,
the soft flesh around my fingertips.
I'd do it on the bus to fifth grade
and then wonder why no cute boy
wanted to hold my hand, pitiful
masochist. At fifteen, it was a boy
who held more than just my hand,
but my heart, aflame, in his pocket.
At twenty, it is perfume and candles
and houseplants. My windowsill
brims with succulents and seasonal
mums and I tend to them like small
children. It's the end of the world
but playing the role of careful mother
offers the almost-believable illusion
that we are not as doomed as we feel.

Praise be to the things that grow.

Praise be to the obsessions we grow
with and then out of, our dead skin
and dead names and overwatered
plants, still clinging to life somehow.

Eighth Grade

When we weren't looking we grew up—and out
of homecoming parades and school bus field trips
and first-ever crushes, penning *I like you* on loose-leaf
paper to slip into the vents of our steel lockers.
If you asked me to the dance, just know I'd say yes.
Curling iron years, learning how to seem cool
and aloof over text, hurling our phones across
the room at sleepovers, masking racing hearts,
Shirley Temples in disposable cups. We were
anything but cool and aloof. I memorized,
with a serial killer's talent, the scent of his
laundry detergent as he passed me before
the homeroom bell. I wanted him forever.
One day I'll marry him, I remember thinking,
over-lining my eyes with sparkling turquoise.
He never asked me to the dance, but I found

I hardly cared. The school cafeteria erupted
in blue light, DJ mixing *Billboard*'s Top 100,
the first week of June 2014, and I danced until
I had to kick off my kitten heels and after that
danced some more. I held my best friend's hand
through the slow songs. I remember how we lost
our voices shrieking the cheesy lyrics, shutting
our eyes and not looking and growing up.

Bildungsroman

I grew up on Sunday night youth group playing Sardines behind the Catholic parish chapel under suburban stars. We used to intentionally hide in storage closets so we could sit with our crushes in dark stillness, bodies innocently pressed against ceiling-high stacks of metal folding chairs. It was the age of giddy purity. My coming-of-age story was written in brick red drugstore lipstick and thrifted prom dresses I wore to my first real boyfriend's homeschool parties. It was the age of Sylvia Plath's *The Bell Jar* and Arctic Monkeys and baby pink Converse high-tops muddied by hometown soil. Of uneven side bangs cut with safety scissors and sucking in my stomach at the ballet barre in that pale yellow room with mirrored walls. Back then I believed in everything and nothing. I wanted to be sought after but not seen. I was a good girl pining for faraway cities and freedom from my seventeenth year. I wrote my college applications in free verse poetry and shrugged my shoulders at every rejection letter. I trained my mouth to memorize the vocabulary of bad girls. At the time I envisioned my future self finally content in a New York apartment, some prestigious writing school, marrying someone who would teach me to outgrow my sweetness. Someone who would teach me how to live. I never quite reached those dreams but in retrospect they were good to have. I covered every inch of my bedroom wall with magazine cutouts of body parts I found beautiful. Elbows and lips and glittery eyes. I didn't know it then but this was my attempt to assemble for myself a body I felt safe in. I can still feel my heart racing, crouching behind the back door of the church, half-hoping to be found so the game would end.

Nesting Doll

I store every small life I've lived inside of me like a nesting doll, layer by layer, each a dreamy variation of the next. Outermost: linen sheets, the warm glow of summer painting my bare back, patchouli and vetiver on my wrists. This is the one I wear now.

Crack me open. Peer in. You'll find a starry universe of becoming.

The next layer—I could never be ashamed of it. It is painted in the colors of my hometown: the scent of fenced-in barbecues at twilight, my first love's laughter, anger at God in church pews. Here, I wear fishnets and write about needing to scream in a town that would never forgive me if I did. I am untethered, hardly there.

Keep going. There is endless goodness within. You will find me in patent leather ballet shoes, fingertips stained from art class, innocent enough to believe in the wickedness of calling someone *stupid*. I take care of earthworms and I'll sing every song I know over voicemails to my parents' friends. I pray with my eyes closed.

It's strange to me—that you will only ever touch the shell I wear now, that you only know me by the perfume I wear, the presence of my laughter, and twenty years of stories still tragically untold. Just patchouli and vetiver, sun on my shoulder blades, and skin.

My Last Day as a Child

written the night before my 18th birthday

is not today.

Even after my roots silver,
bones melted to wax, birthday candles
long since sacrificed for sleep,

I will still be dizzy light and altitude,
propped upon my father's shoulders,
chasing the cobalt shore, fitting my feet
inside his bigger prints.

Still a baby-faced stickler for perfection:
wretched eyesight, hunched over
clicking typewriter keys bleeding poetry
from the tips of gentle fingers.

I will still be seventeen and ablaze,
bleaching hair rebellion red,
intoxicated by forehead kisses
on rainy Saturday past-midnights,
safety in split ends and sadness.

Not today.

No abrupt finalities here.

Today is a day for feet crunching
in the shed skin of autumn leaves,
for giggling like a kindergartner
at playground recess that never ends.

My last day as a child will be the last day of my life,
not the eve of my eighteenth revolution around the sun.
She still has enough light to lift me up on tall shoulders,
just as my father did on those windswept sands of time,
receding to oblivion.

Beat on, young heart.

Breathe flame.

You still have far too many lives left to live.

Far too many to claim
forever yours.

Still Walking Home

I am dreaming of a certain place and time and it is neither here nor now. Tonight, I am eighteen again. Lorde's *Melodrama* overwhelms the wires of my headphones as I walk home from the most hated dining hall on campus with a carry-out box of lukewarm Chinese noodles. It's October, and the leaves have yet to turn, and it's just rained in the typical Southwest Virginia fashion: sudden downpour followed by perfect, holy stillness. I'm making every effort to step gracefully into every puddle, rubber rain boots tiptoeing across the wet, starlit pavement. Wandering alone at night is a kind of prayer, I realize at this moment. Loneliness is perfect company; it'll talk back to you if you let it. Here in the blue, rolling mountains, I am capable of dreaming in a way my retired suburbia could never permit. The energy always sickened me: gridlock, depressed commuters, pollution of the air and mind. It's just different here. Tomorrow I'll call my mom and tell her I want to get my PhD in poetry someday because my most intimidating professor told me I had *a terrifying knack for unleashing beauty*. I'll take the transit bus to nowhere with a new friend of mine and let her convince me to adopt a betta fish for my dorm room. I'll send a handwritten letter to the boy I adored and left behind for a new world unfit for the two of us to remain tethered at the hip. I don't know what I'll end up writing yet. *I miss you* sounds too much like *I miss home*, as if the sentiments are interchangeable, which I cannot say with integrity. Maybe I'll ramble on about how I'm trying to become a vegetarian because I care too deeply about the cows I pass when I stroll through the golden pastures, or that I've been sucking at making it to Sunday mass, or that I'm letting myself be impulsive with someone who *wants* (not loves) me because no one's here to tell me I shouldn't mess with hands as greedy as his. In my head I'm still walking home, inebriated by dense autumn air and life itself. I know the noodles will be awful. But it doesn't matter, because I'm turning nineteen in three weeks, and I'm seriously considering getting my nose pierced like the cool girls in my literature classes, and tonight my loneliness does more than just talk back—it sings.

Bedroom Collection 2/2

I.

Damp air, mold and mildew, paper-thin facades leaving nothing to the imagination. Even with the door locked and secured by electronic keypad prone to malfunction I knew exactly what so-and-so did last Friday night with an upperclassman she met while inebriated at one of the more notorious fraternity houses. Alpha something or other. I didn't even have to ask; I heard. In that room we left the windows gaping wide in the dead of winter. The air never moved, only churned like a sick stomach.

II.

T and I weren't really friends but then we were and then we weren't and then we finally were, for real the last time. In our corners, snapshots of past lives. Boyfriends. High school theatre performances. Smiling faces of hearts we had to leave behind. How comical, what humidity and homesickness and hardly a 10×10 expanse of cheap tile floor can do to two girls. We grew insane in there as our photos, Scotch-taped and secured, plummeted from the sweating wall. Sad fate. Nothing stuck. It was a home we tried to make a home but never really became a home, no matter how many

times we rearranged the furniture at 3 a.m. in hopes of
changing the energy of that blessed, cursed lack of space.

III.

When she left for good I stayed behind and felt
strange inside, the room barren and stripped of noise,
of Kacey Musgraves's *Golden Hour* on loop from her side of
the room, the wafting scent of burnt cookies from the kitchen
next door, the volleyball court view usually obstructed by
window box fans, our end-of-day talking half-asleep about
who we ran into, the clumps of hair we found in the sticky
communal showers, the rowdy boys down the hall always
yelling about unimportant things, everything and nothing.

IV.

Suddenly it was May and the world smelled of flowers
blooming in sidewalk cracks and it was time to leave forever.
Out came the rags and the floor cleaner and away went the
remnants of my first year, clothes folded and crammed back
into the car trunk they hailed from. It was the end of spring
and my soul twinged, having left behind the first place I ever
dreamt of forgetting. We were there and then we weren't.

V.

I pass it sometimes. Familiar limestone and brick. Still,
it's not the same. We no longer haunt. No more of our tears
fall within the cement walls of the sacred profane, no more
constant hum, heat never rising, song of summer stuck
in the throat. That damp air belongs to someone else now.

VI.

It changed us, though.
It changed us.

How I Know There's a Part of Me That Still Feels

When my father paints over the bubblegum pink walls of my childhood bedroom, I have to look away. It's as if we are burying a living thing, ignoring the rise and fall of a heaving chest, hiding a fresh corpse from eager scavengers. I think of everything that particular shade of pink has seen. Wild cousin laughter and fumbled guitar chords and futile first attempts at love poetry. Bad boyfriends and pretty good ones and ghosts of a younger body hunched over a sticky-keyed typewriter. That shade of pink knows me better than I do, has witnessed every slip into madness and every rare moment of peace. But there's a flickering like grace even in the undoing. There's an air of calm in the deconstruction of a past that no longer flatters a frame like mine.

I buried a friend today.

I loved her but it was time.

4:06 PM

I took my first breath then.

My mother can still resurrect that afternoon as crisp as new.
One of those perfect November days, sixty-four degrees
and cloudy with a chance of hope. That sacred autumn cool
where all there is to do is wait for something to happen.
So that's just what she did. She waited for me like prayer.

For years, I'd wait for the exact moment she waited for
to blow out my candles. I couldn't even consider myself
an entire year older until the minute hand reached the time
I was born into this new world of being *daughter,* 4:06 PM,
baby pink in my father's arms, no longer just *idea,*
or mere *possibility,* or even *the dream come true,*
she will be born healthy, she will be born girl,
until the instance of magic
I felt her hands for the first time
and became not just *daughter,* but *theirs.*

Sometimes, even on days that are not my birthday,
just normal drowsy afternoons with nothing left to do
but wait for the sound of something sweet to fill the air,
I just breathe. All over again, like prayer—

taking it all in as if for the first time.

II

Ghost Stories

Church Street

You'd walk with me to therapy. I'd constantly reassure you that I was capable of getting there alone. After all, the lady was kind. Her office, a couple blocks from campus, was decorated in comforting shades of purple. She diffused delicious essential oils (usually lemongrass, sometimes lavender), and the entire practice was situated at the top of a pillared mansion, up the cascading staircase, first door to the right. I knew I'd manage without you. But you didn't care, you knew I secretly preferred it, having a companion to fool around with before pouring my trauma out on a silver platter for her to examine and dissect. On the way there, we'd stop for spicy Chinese noodles, burn our tongues trying to shove it all down quickly enough to make it to the appointment on time, and then jaywalk (more like jay*sprint*) across the busy street to beat the idle traffic light.

We were usually alone in the waiting room, watching the sun burn the telephone wires of our small town the color of a ripe apricot. I'd schedule my appointments late to avoid the rush hour of other college students waiting to get their respective brains "fixed." I'd make faces at you from behind whatever dog-eared, ragged copy of *Good Housekeeping* I could find, feigning pornographic bedroom eyes just to make you laugh. *You're a temptress,* you'd say half-jokingly. But that's exactly what I was doing, tempting you to need me.

My therapist had a name for you: *your friend in the waiting room.* She'd pop her head out to call my name and wave to you, knowing you'd be there, one leg coolly folded on your knee, working on homework balanced like a trapeze artist. Inside the room with the door shut, I'd bombard her with the usual pain: my characteristic loss of friends (inevitable, and always my fault), my abandonment issues, and my unforgiving hostility toward my family for cursing me with the genetics that made me want to kill myself. She'd listen and offer empathy. One night, after our session ended, I had one hand on the doorknob before she stopped me. *Is that sweet boy in the waiting room your boyfriend?* I wanted to say, *He used to be.* I wanted to say, *Kind of.* But instead I said, *No, he's just my friend,* which wasn't a lie, but wasn't a full truth either. *Well,* she replied with a scarecrow-like smile pasted on her face, *You're lucky to have someone like him.*

And I was.

I break out in cold sweat thinking about walking to see her again. I've been putting it off, cancelling appointments, faking soundness of mind just to avoid walking past our token Chinese restaurant with the sticky booths and the chain of mom-and-pop stores perfect for mindless window shopping and the pedestrian light that never turns and Church Street—fittingly named for the Baptist, Presbyterian, Episcopal, Methodist, and Lutheran churches standing stoically one after another like dominoes—where we'd test the door handles of each building hoping one would let us in. It was stupid fun. But you've grown tired of me, and you despise me now, which just means that no one's gonna walk me there if I ever muster enough courage to walk back. No one's gonna sit for a full hour in the waiting room just to take the transit bus with me after sunset so I wouldn't have to ride alone. No one's gonna ask me how it went—*Did you tell her about your parents? How do you feel?*—or squeeze my hand in the dark when it went terribly, the nights I'd dive a little too deeply into my hurt. You were my friend. You held my hand. I didn't know it then, but I needed you.

She'll ask me, *Where's your friend?* And I'll shrug my head and say something like *Not here,* or *Probably just busy,* because I'll talk about anything to anyone—my twisted history, my constant suffering, my wounds that won't heal—but I won't talk about Church Street, or how all of the church doors were bolted shut, or how I wanted to kiss you on the way back, like old times, but didn't.

Holy Whatevers

Chipped coffee mugs half-filled with cheap liquor,
makeshift blanket forts, a locked door. Lipstick
rubs off when I scrub my lips in the shower
but guilt does not; it sits like a sore and festers.
I started to believe in the permanence of those
holy whatevers: paresthetic leg under the weight
of you, static electricity, the pins and needles
of knowing someone almost fully. I say almost
because we never really do. No matter how
easy it becomes to sacrifice sanity, how natural
it becomes to wear each other's smiles like
sweatshirts in a too-hot September, there is more
to a person than who they were when they left.
I thought you were composed of magic, under your
skin a gleam of nirvana; if anyone asked me I could
have sworn you were a god in another hourglass.
Those sacred trivialities: strands of my hair
on your perfumed pillowcase, arguments about
the universe under halcyon skies, a litany
of touching and colliding. The whole world
would call us blasphemy, would deem us sinful.

But I kept my toothbrush in your medicine
cabinet. I kicked your leg in my nightmares.
When you pick your lip, does it still bleed?

Or Current Resident

Chinese Kitchen on North Main has been alive longer than I have. *26th Anniversary, 15% off* boasts curly lettering, origin Microsoft Word. I am stunned by the permanence of things. Last winter an old friend of mine used to peer into the misty shop window with me, watching locals passionately devour steamed dumplings. We swore we'd try them one day but never got around to it. Dear Current Resident of Apartment E, take this booklet of coupons, for *Big Easy Savings, Priced Low Every Day.* If only they knew I wish I could buy time. That I wish I could fill my plate with heaps of minutes, that I wish we could have been permanent enough to make it inside. Maybe we would've loved their sesame chicken, or maybe we'd come back over and over for the house special, or the beef lo mein or maybe we'd deem it *whatever* and never come back, passing the open sign every night but at least we'd know. I've got a phantom limb taste in my mouth that wouldn't be there if he had just kept walking me home.

I Was Never Peaceful

She makes you tea. Chamomile.
Water first, then leaves. Let steep.
It's the way you've always taken it, the way
I learned from you—water always cardinal.
And then, while heat emancipates itself, she sits
in your lap and blathers philosophy. The origin
of language and ethics and dreams. It's carnal to you.
Enticing. Intellectual lust has always been a weakness.
You are charmed by girls with vagabond minds, at least
you were for me. Or maybe she does it all backwards.
Leaves first, then water. Opposite arrangements.
And maybe she talks about nothing, just rests
her head on your shoulder and waits in perfect peace.
I was never peaceful. I was bold and combustible
and aggravating, I bet. But you adored it.
That I was violently obsessed with
thinking. Sensually aware—
the god of memorizing
your arrangements
and speaking them.

Unfinished Short Stories

Twilight at the tennis court, heartbeats stuck in the mesh, this is how I want to remember you. In exaggerated grunts and lilting laughter, in this scattering half-light you move like an oil painting finished just moments ago. We're clowns, both of us, exaggerating our grunts like the pros on TV do. I run like a fool, serve you the ball, sprint to return it, sky darkening until we can't make out the white lines anymore.

This is how I want to remember you, along with the other vignettes I carousel between in my head. Like origami cranes hung from loft bed frames, too much cologne, a single red rose. My hair stuck in your window fans, turtlenecks in July because you could never help yourself, how we concealed our contrabands: boxed chardonnay, what happened behind the parked tractor, the secrets we'd swap. That one time we went to that psychedelic poetry exhibit with the rotating walls that made us hallucinate for hours, how afterward we lay flat on our backs to trace fake constellations with our pointer fingers, how we'd always walk home stained by grass and drunk on the absurd philosophies we'd invent.

This is how I want to remember you, in these short stories only you know the endings to, but mostly that one night, at the tennis court, when we were clowns and the lines were there, fencing us in, holding us close, until they couldn't.

Great Danes and Tea Bags

I like to imagine you reading my poetry. It's almost sadistic, how desperately I wish to witness your pupils nervously flitting from line to line, configuring words into something resembling *meaning,* occasionally stumbling upon a memory of ours and swallowing hard. I play the reverie over and over in my mind. A blink. A clearing of the throat, then an Adam's apple following shortly behind. Yes, I'm a little sick in the head.

I like to imagine that the act of doing so is something secret, privately profane, only permissible once she falls asleep so there are no questions asked that you can't answer. Like why you care so much about what I have to say, or why you have to wait until two in the morning to tediously unravel what I've made. I like to imagine you killing time until her eyelids flutter shut before finally letting the glow of your screen suffuse your skin. And then you begin, catching glimpses of your face in every "you" I've written.

The images come in brutal flashes. There we are in June, in my car, the wind blowing so ruthlessly I keep choking on my own hair. It's our seventeenth summer. I'm learning how to drive and I hit every curb. You're smoking the cigarettes you stole from your older brother which he stole from your dad. You're laughing at me. You can't look away.

Tonight, you can't look away, either. You sink silently into each aching recollection. That time we almost adopted the Great Dane we didn't have one square foot of space for. How you'd tie tea bag strings around my ring finger, promising me the whole world.

In the morning she'll kiss you awake and ask how you slept. And you'll say *It was fine*. But you won't mention how stealthily you had to cry, careful not to disturb her peace.

To Tell You the Truth

I was banking on forever.

Carving pumpkins with you the day after Halloween, pulps already rotting, you'd stick your slender fingers into that cavernous decay and laugh like a serial killer.

I secretly loved it, watching your jack-o'-lantern smile flicker through slime-covered hands. Stupid kid, you. Sometimes I loved you so much I wanted to hurt you.

I know I did in the end.

Do you remember our belated Halloweens as vividly as I do? And our makeshift birthday parties, just us and two slices of store-bought wedding cake rejects. Our Christmases, even though you couldn't grasp the concept of Jesus and hated commercialization, how we'd unwrap each other's gifts and feign surprise. I liked to trick myself into thinking you knew me less than you actually did. How it kept the mystery alive, kept you intrigued enough to keep undoing me, but

to tell you the truth

I was banking on forever.

I still don't know how to *Halloween*
or *holiday* or *pretend that I don't wish
I still did.* It's almost October and if
someone were to peer through my skin,
they'd find that nothing glows, no light,
just a faint flicker if you trick yourself
long enough to believe in ghost stories.

It Was Never About Tea

Ballpoint poems on chewing gum wrappers,
my words a brisk mint dancing on your tongue.
I'd slip them inside your notebooks to unfold
on harder days, writing you into a new world
when your real one would crumble. We used
to make tea and then forget to drink it. Now
I realize it was not forgetfulness, but our own
vernacular. There, in the cooling steam, was
our way of sharing understanding, letting
each other steep in these invented routines.
Effortless vocabulary: flushed faces, sudden
downpours, blurry snapshots of hip bones
painted by morning light, no need to speak.
Superficial nothings, trifles that glimmer;
when the patterns finally broke so did I.

Persimmons Under Evergreen Trees

The story continues elsewhere—somewhere
no longer habitable—in a secret place
beyond the fringes of bodily reach. I know this to be true
because I can still feel the physical movement
of anatomies ripe with call and response,
weight shifting and unfolding like origami paper,
hidden flesh creasing then collapsing.

The story—*our* story—endures
in the memory of its telling.

In that secret place we are still allowed
to share persimmons under evergreen trees,
spitting seeds into stiff grass, colliding teeth
with nectarous juice still dripping from our lips.

In that secret place we are still allowed
to wash each other's backs,
treating each vertebra like gospel, scrubbing
the peaks and valleys of our earthly forms
until we are made new again.

I know that place exists

because sometimes I wake to the taste of winter fruit
as if I'd bitten into something ripe just seconds ago,
or the sensation of fingers skimming the dips of my spine,
a feeling like coming home.

And I know it's you—

reaching out from that other world we cannot visit
where the story never ends—
and that it has to be you,
because no one moves me the same way, or ever could,

in this one.

Part I: Chapter Endings From a Book I'll Never Write

Alternate titles:

A Collection of Real and Fake Stories: All Involving Hand-Holding

Repressed Trauma, but Make It Art

These Characters Aren't Real, so Stop Guessing

Or Are They? Perhaps Partially

Even in the dim of the theater, I was almost *too* aware of him. I can't precisely describe the hypersensitivity, but it was as if the act of him sitting next to me made his presence an extension of my body. Our hands did that predictable dance you see in coming-of-age movies: dangling off the slimy arm rests, buttery fingers "accidentally" grazing, every tiny shift electric-shocking up my arm. And the next thing you know, he's holding my hand like it's natural—inevitable. It just happens. It feels like dying a thousand oxytocin-fueled deaths, like those *instances of the sublime* you hunt for in English literature. He caresses the dips between my knuckles and I, glowing scarlet, turn to him in that pale cinema light and whisper, *I'm not your fucking piano.* We do that throughout the whole movie. I don't even remember how it ends; that's how overwhelmed I was by his knee weighing against mine, the nectarous smell of him so new and already saturating my lungs. When I got home, I paced my room trying to catch my breath for an hour. I couldn't shower. I just kept looking at the ticket stub, a madwoman unsteady and aching to teleport back to just hours before when I hadn't yet felt the rush of him close to me. I wanted to experience that completely submerged, utterly inundated sinking feeling for the first time again. I still can't cough it out of my lungs.

Part II: Chapter Endings From a Book I'll Never Write

Alternate titles:

A Collection of Real and Fake Stories: All Involving Hand-Holding

Repressed Trauma, but Make It Art

These Characters Aren't Real, so Stop Guessing

Or Are They? Perhaps Partially

Compromised by five different varieties of sketchy juice, S* asked me with bambi eyes if I'd ever, in the history of our casual acquaintance, had "real feelings" for him. Almost too enthusiastically, I said *yes* because how could I not? My feelings were always real, especially with him; in retrospect he should've known that. Thin frame set aflame by the glowing lamp posts outside his window, he ran his index finger down my arm and professed I had the smoothest skin he'd ever touched. Only after the goosebumps formed did he tell me I kissed funny and I lost sleep over that for months, even when I started kissing other people. In the morning, our eyelids fluttered open and he put on *The Edge of Seventeen* and I felt seventeen, the kind of seventeen I never got to live.

I clutched his hand and he did mine and I thought he was into me, that to him I was as sound as gospel. But he dropped me off after sunrise, hurriedly mumbling something along the lines of *see ya around* and left me pondering, yearning for days. The next day, a text: *I have your necklace. It's on my nightstand. You left it behind.* I told no one about it.

But I didn't care about the necklace. I wished I could've left more of me behind. I wished he had loved me, even just for a little bit, an afternoon or an evening or even just in a sentence. For a few hours I felt like his stereotypical indie film girlfriend, the one who'd write poetry about his dark eyes and dark hair and how he wasn't my type but that didn't matter, only because it's him. I could be his manic pixie dream girl for good. I imagined meeting his mom, sitting on his family couch, resting my head on his dog's stomach, flipping through the plastic album sleeves of his baby books. Who does that after a failed affair? I can't watch *The Edge of Seventeen* anymore. I can't think about that window view, or of "real feelings" and all of the light waking us up and me silently begging *stay, stay asleep just a little while longer, don't walk me home, not now, not yet, not ever.*

*S: redacted. His name doesn't even start with an S. He might not even be real. Stop guessing.

Part III: Chapter Endings From a Book I'll Never Write

Alternate titles:

A Collection of Real and Fake Stories: All Involving Hand-Holding

Repressed Trauma, but Make It Art

These Characters Aren't Real, so Stop Guessing

Or Are They? Perhaps Partially

On his nightstand: fifteen orange pill bottles lined up like plastic soldiers ready for war, a marble guitar pick nearly bent in half, an empty dream journal, and above it all, a gaping hole in the drywall from the night I told him all of it was too much for me. I hated holding his hand. It felt like clutching something clinging to life by a thinning thread, a run-over animal laboring for its last breaths. "Come closer," he'd say, but closer was everywhere I couldn't stand to be. His room reeked of grief, of months-unwashed sheets and sour sickness and my foolish inability to relate. His pain was fragrant and all I could do was soak in it, graceless. He only praised my poetry when it bled. I think this was his way of entertaining a pent-up fantasy of us taking over the world, one miserable line at a time. I never kissed him, not even on his good days. I was too afraid that, by loving him even slightly, I'd kill him. But I think that's what I did anyway, albeit in a different way, killed him so good he ended up writing seven awful songs with my first name plastered right there in the titles. I listened to them secretly, hearing him curse me under dissonant guitar chords, those bedroom lullabies damning me to hell. For months I wondered why. Was it because I couldn't stomach the portrait of him: unkempt, rageful, defeated? That I couldn't mask my discomfort under the ballads I'd write for him? That I never knew what to say when he wept over his own survival? And then I remembered. I had penned a letter: *I can't love you the way you want me to*. It was only after I arrived home, after slipping it into his unzipped backpack, that I realized. It was his birthday.

Every Time I See Someone Who Walks Like You

I hold my breath. From across the empty soccer field by our apartment complex on Wednesday afternoon I could have sworn I saw the exact outlines of a body I used to memorize by heart—slender-legged, poor posture, meandering through the chemically treated grass with no sense of direction. You used to pace the forest *just thinking. About what?* I'd ask you, after you'd disappear for hours without warning. *Nothing really,* you'd say, and shrug your shoulders far too casually for me to believe. But those nights, playing with your pale blond baby hairs and forcing you to guess the words I'd write sloppily on your back with my fingertips (*the answer was always I love you*) I didn't feel the need to know what you were thinking. It's funny how *Nothing really* suffices until it doesn't. Until I'm squinting my eyes from a hundred feet away, wondering if the dimensions of the wandering man match yours. But the mathematics are always a little bit skewed. He's either too tall or not tall enough, sporting an outfit you'd never wear. *Tell me, do you ever try to find me in the shadows of other people? Do you hold your breath until you're wrong, too?*

Main Street

There are over 10,000 Main Streets in the United States of America. They're scattered everywhere. Focal points of Christmas card townships, city corners, college campuses. You can envision a Main Street in your mind without even needing to visit one: strings of charming gift shops, a historic post office, probably a dilapidated dry cleaning service or two with boarded-up windows. I must confess, I am pathetically in love with the self-righteous importance of Main Streets. They're not just *streets*, but capital M *Main Street*s. Every local knows which street you're talking about. *The only one that really matters around here.*

I can't walk down the Main Street we knew anymore because that's just something that happens when you love someone and they leave. You start taking the long way home, even when the sun sets and you'd theoretically be much safer as a woman walking under Main Street's lampposts rather than traversing the unlit, soulless alleyways. You start walking past Main Street without letting your eyes flit left or right, because you know that you'll see them—*them*—those young, red-faced couples standing at the corner, waiting for the pedestrian light to turn. If I look a little too long, the girl in the red coat becomes me. She's wiping the fog from the boy's clear-rimmed glasses with her scarf like I did for you.

Maybe one day I'll be brave enough to stand at that light alone until it turns. Maybe I'll walk to the coffee shop where we used to order spicy chai in late October and watch the hungover college kids meander through the farmers market, toting around loaves of sourdough bread and orange wildflowers through unrelenting nausea. I'll have no one to laugh at them with but the tea would be just as sweet. I'll just have to make it work.

There are over 10,000 Main Streets in the United States of America but *only one that matters* to me. It's the one nestled in the heart of Southwest Virginia, where we'd peer into the high-end clothing stores and pretend we could afford the outfits on the window mannequins. It's the one where we snuck into that record store and I went home with miscellaneous hits from the 1960s, Bonnie Tyler, *Jesus Christ Superstar*, and Vivaldi's *The Four Seasons*. That was the day we ran to the bus stop in the rain, your socks drenched and hair glued to your forehead and I knew it. *I could never love anyone like this again.*

On Main Street I watched your eyes fill with rain as you sang *Happy Birthday* to me over chocolate cheesecake. On Main Street we shared blood orange sorbet on the bench and watched the usual crowd of night revelers stumble into bars. On Main Street we joked about being married college professors like the ones we'd spot at the underrated sushi place. On Main Street we thought it would all work out.

Maybe one day I'll stop taking the long way home.

Eighth Wonder of the Apartment Kitchen

I keep thinking about the time I tried to convince you that substituting olive oil for the vegetable oil I had forgotten to toss into my grocery cart earlier that day would work perfectly fine for the recipe. *It's just oil*, I shrugged. *And ginger snaps are spicy enough to mask the difference, anyway.* Leaning over the kitchen counter, slumped in your usual posture, you shook your head omnisciently and promised me it wouldn't. *Just trust me*, you said. But I've always been stubborn—especially with you—so I ignored your rash foreshadowing and poured the pale green liquid until it spilled over the edge of the measuring cup. Into the batter it settled. You smiled as I relished in my own genius, twirling in circles, a kitchen fairy.

When the oven beeped, our cookies had turned a repulsive shade of beige. The texture and flavor reeked of my poor judgment. As I disgustedly dumped the contents of the tray into the disposal, I remember taking note of the depth of your stare—half pure fascination, half all-knowing. You were certain I wouldn't listen; I hardly ever did. You just wanted to observe me, annoyingly persistent and forever set in my ways. In your eyes I was the Eighth Wonder of the Apartment Kitchen.

I should've heeded your advice about the oil. And then again, when you warned me through sticky tears that the man I would eventually leave you for would squander me like a counterfeit, like a lousy batch. If I were a real genius of foresight, I would've saved the batter for tomorrow.

I'd siphon it into Tupperware until I could buy a cheap bottle of the proper oil. We'd just bake tomorrow.

Maybe I'd even stay with you, instead of fleeing from the only person who cared enough to adore me, even in the failure of my own false prophecy.

To be observed like that by another soul again. To be understood and adored—*just trust me*—before the timer went off and it was time to reveal what we had made.

Dead Rain

Soaked by sudden storm, rain saturating the apples
of our cheeks, there was a time for dripping hair.
You and I, howling while running for shelter.
And after drying each other's shivering figures,
making soup. There was a time for that, too,
warming numb faces against steaming bowls,
letting the blood return, painting us pink again.

But time does not keep
and cannot endure.
It must make room for other downpours,
new bodies to fill its vacancies, fresh forms.

I run with someone else now, and before the sky pours
we're already home. But sometimes,
when there is no water to wring from my clothes
and my hair still looks the way it did when I left
I remember making soup, heat rising calmly
to meet us, all of our leaking laughter—
you and your still-wet smile.

Perfect Incompletions

I lent you

weak-spined paperback books, coins for your bus fare home,
the defenselessness of my body in late September, eager
silhouettes playing against peeling paint and dying light.

You lent me

halves of your sandwiches, chronicles from childhood,
the nape of your neck where I would trace my name
with my lips to make you appear more real
to me, more conscious.

I liked to imagine
shaping you with my palms
like some sort of maniacal artist.
As if you were my pottery, my life's work,
that I could mold you however I saw fit,
keeping you on the wheel
to be governed by my movements.

But the body is not clay
and nor is it soulless.
It cannot spin forever.
It does not defy inertia.

With you I learned
that the body is only lent in intervals
and then taken back after it is due.
I thought I'd have my whole life
to sculpt you without flaw, but you,
my almost-magnum opus,
are my holy unfinished.

If This Is It

Remember me happy. Remember me a giggling wild thing nuzzled into the freckled bend of your elbow. Remember me dancing, mandarin orange peels in both hands, under the soft overhead light of your apartment kitchen. Remember me flailing my arms to our song in your car, embarrassing you silly in front of all the others waiting for the light to turn. Remember me chasing your little cousin in that chalked-over driveway, spawning into a monster of his imagination just to hear his wicked childish laughter fill our air. Remember me so in love with you I could've died right there, having lived a full life with nothing else I could've dreamed of needing. There was no poverty with you.

If this is it, remember me sparkling. Remember me spinning in that dress for you, all satin and magic and woman and alive. Remember me cracking jokes with your brothers at dinner, the first summer I met your parents, that April I first wrote of you, for you. Remember me in memories of my kicked-off boots at your front door, my seventh heaven dive under your covers. Remember me intoxicated by hope. The very first time I kissed your cheek, my nineteenth springtime in full bloom, how the pink rising in your face competed with everything blossoming around us. Remember me richly yours. Remember me happy.

Song of Solomon and of Myself

What is the proper way to say
*don't wait for me, for I have found
the one whom my soul loves?*
What is the proper way to pledge
allegiance to a new nation, to emigrate
from the history of self, seeking asylum
from the body you once called home?
What is the proper way to beg God
for new skin? For a waist you never traced,
for bones you never bit? *Jesus, teach me*
how to bleed in reverse, watch the red
pour back into my side, the art
of never being crucified. What is the proper
way to love? Must it always equate
with sacrifice? Is there a way to say *hold me*
without anticipating the wound, to say *take
me* without feeling the lance go in,
and out, and in again?

Don't wait for me, for I have found
the one whom my soul loves.
Teach me love that leaves without a stain.

III

Love Letters

How Great Thou Art

for Andrew and our sweet Appalachia

Mornings in the mountains are to the soul as honey is to a sore throat. I swear I could live like this forever: cheeks stained midwinter pink, quick forehead kisses before the light turns green again, your thumb surfing easy across my knuckles during the Our Father. These are the days we bundle up snowman-style over our Sunday best, giggle in coffee breath, warm our faces over something freshly pulled from the oven. I am infinitely happy beneath these lavender skies, heavens bleeding into our Blue Ridge like a watercolor daydream. It is before the world wakes up. It is after darkness falls. These are mornings straight out of Rockwell paintings, Grimms' Fairy Tales, every biblical creation story translated to any language spoken by tongues like ours. It is said that, after the great design, God observed all He had made and, in splendor, remarked that it was very good. And indeed, very good are these mornings, these afternoons we spend feeling wholesomely crafted and beautifully made, shy and gorgeous creatures in a handmade, homespun world. It is a perfect morning for almost-perfect loving and I am stitched back together—by smiling babies, your dizzy laughter, our off-key singing all the way back home. These are mornings neither before nor after. Just now, just ours.

You Make Me Want to Say Yes

to orchid centerpieces and crawling ivy
and space to dance. To heels with a crisp
click to them, a white lace A-line dress,
perhaps even some tulle, that perfect swing
of fabric when you dip me into moonlight.
You make me want to become acquainted
with champagne toasts and fine china,
my left hand sporting a heavier finger.
You make me want to *I do* myself
to death. I had never before pictured
becoming that kind of woman, that
specific breed of bold. But for you,
I do. You make me want to be that kind
of almost-summer afternoon, early June,
never lovelier. You make me want to meet
you at the end of every aisle—whether
it be church or grocery store or dilapidated
classroom building. *I do I do I do.*
Meet me there, will you? Meet me
at the intersection of now and always.
You make me want to say yes
to everything in-between.

Nothing Else

Light plays on the ridges of your collarbones
and I have determined that I love you most
fast asleep, a human prism painted by morning.
This moment, I want to preserve it for the rest of time:
your chest rippling in waves, cresting and crashing
under an overcast Saturday sky, acoustic guitar swelling
from my next-door neighbor's apartment kitchen radio.
I wonder where sleep takes you. Am I with you, there?
Or are your dreams wild and boyish, full of outgrown
aggression and muddy knees and brutal brotherhood?
Me, I dream of nothing else but this warm light
and how it chisels you, melting your features
into marble, an act of practical worship.
Nothing else but steady breathing,
this morning, faint music.

Genesis

When God finished shaping the earth,
I wonder if His hands, still caked in clay,
trembled at the sight of something so new.

I imagine Him wiping the dew from his brow,
a soft sigh escaping into the starlight.
Nothing will ever be the same again,
He must have thought, as He perfected Man
and left him, sound asleep, to wake in Paradise.

And I only wonder this because I, too, tremble
feeling the precious weight of your hand in mine.
Something about the way you squeeze back
when I do reminds me of creation.
Genesis is found in the streaks of your irises,
safe blue, treacherous blue, same blue,
same feeling He must have felt
looking down into His new ocean
and weeping for the first time.

Nothing will ever be the same again,
I thought. And nothing was,

and ever will be, with you.

This Will Be Our Year

Somewhere spilling down the winding roads of western Pennsylvania I am with you and we are happy. I've got a good feeling about this one —Christmas lights still wrapped around the pillars of front porches, laughter so sickly sweet it burns, how we are the protagonists of our very own vintage Hallmark special. This year it's too warm for any real snow. It hardly matters, even for people like us, people who love the cinema of a perfect winter. I could do this forever, could call you home for a lifetime, *my place my person my hand to squeeze doesn't matter if we're three-hundred miles from the world I grew up in. I'll just build a new one with you.* I've got a good feeling about being twenty on the first day of this new decade, one as fresh as the winter snow blanketing someone else's front yard in another universe, not ours. Ours is warmed by the little mysteries that lie ahead, waiting for us around the corner to find them, for our hands to unwrap the *will be, one day*, beautiful unknown. Who knows what roads we'll traverse this year or the next, what seeds of love or laughter we will plant, what will become of these stoplight moments, this sunset magic, our midnight slow dances glowing. All I know is that this could be our year. This could be our life, this equitable arrangement of you and me, this could be the world we will keep.

Portrait of Paradise

To my right, a setting sun, sinking behind the rooftops.
To my left, a sleeping boy, face painted by her colors.

I could wake him and put on a record—
Vivaldi: The Four Seasons, perhaps—

yet I do not. In the spaces of our shared silences breathes
something sacred, something reminiscent of the Garden.
He is bathed in orange, cast in gold, shadowed by clouds,
yet wholly unaware of how desperately I wish I could
stop daylight from vanishing, how tragic this brevity.

These are moments to which words cannot hold a candle.

And music, though I live for melody filling the air,
would only stain and ruin the perfection of *now*.

I do not wake him. I let the vinyls rest.

And I, too, rest, letting the Artist do the work.

Juxtaposition

A lot of things simply cannot exist together.

Cats and bubble baths.
Paperback books and spilled glasses of milk.
Love and dishonesty.
Innocence and knowledge.

The universe demands that these sets of objects
remain separate, uninvolved with each other,
divorced from all possible contact.
It is the universal law of long-distance relationships.
To intermingle them would be
to create chaos, to toy with dangerous flame.

But yet some things are made to exist together.

Sidewalk cracks and yellow dandelions.
Buttered popcorn and cinema screens.
Two sets of eager lips.
Your heart, a hummingbird
fluttering in my hands—
I knew from the moment it landed
that it was meant to live there.

I live for the things

you would not expect to exist together.
For the unexpected perfect fit—
two wrongs lining up to make a right,
opposites not only attracting, but
making sweet love out of the very
conflict of existence.

You and I.
I never expected to love you.

But I do.

I love you like waking up early
and accidentally stumbling upon sunrise.
Like random chance.
Like snow in October.
Like coming home after years
of searching everywhere to find it.
And you clutch in your hands a red carnation
so bright against the gray September rain
it could have been mistaken for fire.

Holy Ground

requires no great pilgrimage
nor any red-eye flight to book.
Upon arrival, there may not even
be an altar on which to offer
what is owed.

Holy ground is wherever you leave your love.

So every public bathroom stall within
which I have grieved into my hands.
A certain Catholic church basement,
still haunted by the sweaty magic of old
friends long gone, the dark wooded backroads
of my native Virginia, the humid shoebox room
I occupied my first year apart from childhood,
the grimy twin XL and cobwebbed window panes.

Holy ground is wherever love finds you again.

The back stairwell of the dilapidated classroom
building we accidentally followed last February.
The bus stop where I first kissed you, feeling
it was right. Holy ground, these moonlit paths
I walk with you, wordless, basking in starry stillness,
this sacred earth something we now share.

The Cosmos Is a Romantic

I know so.

Consider the unspoken magnetism between two strangers.
Mystery charges the distance between separate bodies,
interrupting the graceful orbit between planets
never meant to collide.

All love is merely push and pull.
Potential either used or wasted.
Like energy, it cannot be created nor destroyed.
This is the great tragedy of our species, a law of our universe:
sometimes love only lasts the duration of a subway ride,
eye contact for the smallest of eternities, shared laughter
already ancient history seconds after it begins.
We can never get it back, restored to the same version,
the resurrection of a moment in full technicolor detail.
What we reimagine is never enough.
Past realities cannot be resuscitated.
We cannot breathe life into the dead.

This is not purely science, mathematical equations, theories.
It can't be.

The cosmos is a romantic.
I know because we exist.

Inventors

I live by maps and love by stars.
Find the patterns, trail his footsteps,
follow lovers back to their homes.
Feed me sequence: *crack an egg,*
pour the flour, beat until light.
There are roles to play. Everyone
you meet is an archetype of another.
Thinking this way, I am only
an amalgamation of everything
I've seen. Hollywood starlets
of black-and-white films. Pretty
smiles on pretty girls with prettier
minds. There is no such thing
as an authentic original. Every idea
is an act of deflowering. I can try
but I only end up infringing
on someone else's copy. You
and I—we didn't invent romance.
Neither did Juliet and her dagger
or any man holding a boombox
over his head to win the girl.
But God, when you make me
break every rule I've ever written,
it sure feels a lot like we did.

The Good Flesh Continuing

after Robert Hass

Our bodies are extensions of the universe. Recycled stardust, byproducts of galactic explosions. We were born before time. No wonder we must touch. Hands intertwining, tangling, assuming form. To touch is to counterfeit the feeling of coming home, rearranging our atoms in an order that resurrects the *before* of us— less body, less mortal, less blood. How we used to be mere ripples in the fabric of the infinite, still unironed.

When we touch, it is the closest we get to the oneness of our nature. It is our only map. Each scar of yours I trace with my index finger picks up where our origin story left off. This is how we write ourselves whole again. We touch,

we collide—over and over until our dust remembers why.

Homesick for Another World

after Ottessa Moshfegh

I don't try to relate. There's no use. There are billions of brilliant minds and then there's mine, which is neither brilliant nor dull, but somewhere adrift in the dusky in-between. I'm too much of everything and too little of what actually matters. Too much emotion, too little control of it. Too much panic, too little reason for it. In the company of others, I feel almost alien, as if I possess a quality still unknown to me that repels, that turns heads the other direction out of terror. Like the part of the horror movie before the jump scare, before the killer finds the sleeping starlet talking in her sleep. I'm bug-eyed and awkward and better alone. I'm uncomfortable in togetherness, unstable in love, nervous no matter whose arms I rest in. In another life I can breathe. I can let peace just be peace, love just be love. I can hold your hand without tensing up when you loosen your grip. I can speak loud enough for your friends to hear me, can order my own food at the restaurant, can small-talk any stranger. And I'm jealous of the other kinds of minds—minds that would not willingly choose death over being known—jealous of the souls that sparkle without dreading the burden of being seen. I love cold wind that numbs the fingertips and the corners of bustling train stations perfect for poetry and being comfortably alone with you. I love indoor cats observing passersby through the windows of my parochial universe and rundown beach boardwalk shops with the terribly sexist

T-shirts and squeezing your hand in the passenger seat. I love that you love me in spite of my fear of being loved. And that you stay with me, when I'm choking on air, and my mind becomes a haunted house, and I'm weeping in the spare room of your family beach house because the world is too loud for my liking, and I'm one breakdown away from a hospital stay. That you choose me, that you choose me, that you choose me—when I'm homesick for another world but this is the only one we'll ever know.

I Am No Angel

but the woman who loves you.

As far removed from celestial as the word itself permits.
No divine messenger shrouded in starlight, nothing sinless
nor unstained. I do not speak their language of perfect holiness,
that mocking, heavenly song. I am no angel.

I have never fallen from those great heights. Love,
this flesh, do you feel its wickedness, pregnant with earth?
When you taste me, do I leave your tongue marred with soil?
These shoulder blades never grew wings, refusing,
no matter how many nights my small frame crumpled
in prayer for them. I have never indulged in flight or freedom,
have never rescued a soul in peril. The closest I have ever come
is this act of clutching you, sweet being, these mortal arms
warming your bones with the beat of my heart,
all blood and evil ancestry, my love
a clot that holds.

I am no angel, precious thing, but in these finite human moments
in which we are animals keeping warm, nothing but fallible material,
newborn creatures yet to be washed from the origin of our birth
and still fresh from the hidden womb, I come close,

my love, I come close.

Maybe I Would Pixelate

I like to talk about things
like whether or not God would have friends
if He went to my old high school
and how all saints were probably secret skeptics
with blasphemous diary entries and how
I'd rather choke to death than marry someone stupid.

You don't.

You'd rather listen, absorbing my farfetched philosophies,
nodding just to gratify my sickness. I get too swept away in passion,
but you find it charming or exotic or something, I'm still not sure—
but you haven't left yet and that's what makes you different
from everyone else. You tolerate,
at the very least, my diatribes and ramblings, my red-in-the-face
awakenings that leave me breathless and defeated
on your bedroom carpet, muttering *Holy shit* over and over again
into my hands like litany. You don't articulate your opinions
on whether the universe is benevolent or indifferent or evil,
or if you believe money is merely a social construct
invented to control us like I do,
or if you're even remotely afraid of dying.

I used to hate it, and wished that you'd get bloodthirsty for answers
like me, violent for truth palpable enough to hold in your palms.

But now I understand you'd rather just hold me, would rather
just swaddle me in stillness, or maybe you're afraid
that if you verbalized your inner world mine would disintegrate,
that I'd fracture into a thousand pieces, that maybe I would pixelate
in your arms. You don't say much but you don't have to.

I can feel what you're thinking without words,

when you pull me closer, into the act which requires no explanation,
no language, no absurd fit of anger to express its depths.
In these moments you're not thinking about God or money
or really anything at all—other than how to keep me
from swimming too far from shore.

Consider This a Love Letter

to the way your clothes smell after a full day:
sweat, almond-scented body wash, detergent—

to the way you cannot sleep without twitching—

to the pale white scar on your left eyebrow from
falling out of bed as a hyperactive three-year-old—

to your middle child mind—

to the way you sing in falsetto to make me laugh
and the worst part is, it's not even half bad!—

to the yellow bridges that populate the skyline
of the city where you grew up—

to the God you believe in—

to your annoying tendency to listen selectively—

to the way you can't dance
and yet choose to dance with me anyway—

to all of the ways
you are—

IV

Book of Revelation

In Memory of Dreams

In loving memory of those we lost to the Virginia Tech shootings on April 16, 2007. May our beloved Hokies live on forever.

1.

And the feet that once walked the same paths mine do.

2.

Back when the sixteenth of April was just Monday,

3.

we never had to consider roses or candlelight vigils.

4.

We didn't have to.

5.

Time had not yet fallen from innocence,

6.

still unplucked fruit ripening on the branch

7.

because *things like that* don't happen in *a place like this*

8.

or at least that's what everyone thought

9.

until the *things like that* happened on this very ground

10.

which all of a sudden did not feel solid anymore

11.

and the whole world watched that morning

12.

melt into mourning, into itself,

13.

leaving no words behind

14.

in all of that lacking.

15.

The most honest tragedy of this

16.

was not even the sight of blood

17.

but the anxious mother on the other end of the call

18.

waiting for words to make sense of silence.

19.

It is hard enough to watch your child leave

20.

for something like college, I know.

21.

I saw my mother cry when I packed up my room.

22.

But how do you reconcile that hurt

23.

with the hurt of these mothers:

24.

see you Thanksgiving, Christmas, Easter,

25.

but all of a sudden there were no more days

26.

much less holidays. No coming back home.

27.

How do you learn to set four places at the table instead of five?

28.

How do you smile at stories of other people

29.

living out their dreams, knowing full well

30.

that these thirty-two never got to wake up from theirs?

31.

Every day I wake up here

32.

I realize how much that matters.

This Unearthly Glow

I private-message my poet friend. *I want our world back.*

Almost instantly, she replies. *I want our world back too.*

I say *It feels so different. Something feels changed. Can't pinpoint what. Like energy, a strange invisible movement.*

As if there's been a fundamental shift out in the universe and we are lost in ripples on the outer edge, she responds. Then, something to cleanse the palate. *You'd like Oregon.*

I've always wanted to go there. Very cinematic, I answer. For a moment I dream of somewhere new to me. *But no, I understand. Something cosmic feels terribly misaligned. I've never been this existentially fearful. There's a deep-rooted anxiety that feels weirdly apocalyptic.* I think of Oregon. I think of my poet friend and our old world.

She counters, *Like the calm right before a storm we've never had before. Settled in a state of discomfort.* Then, *I think I'm gonna go cry in the shower now.* I double-tap her message. This is how scared kids express solidarity.

These are the days for standing beneath streams of water and weeping, panicked by what unknown Armageddon might already be crowning. *Corona:* in anatomical terms a part of the body resembling a crown. In astronomical terms, a glowing envelope surrounding our sun and stars.

What blinds our sight? What crowns from our bodies? What surrounds us in this way that cannot be seen nor perceived, this way that leaves poets without language?

So I Let Myself Cry

at the videos of people singing in unison from their balconies
in full belief that only music can stop this war and I let myself
mourn the images of ransacked grocery store aisles, someone's
mother weeping because there's nothing left but new language
called *fear of the unknown* and because we can't clutch hands,
not yet, which is all I need when I wake and the world feels more
like a burning corpse and less like the one we remember and so
I let my heart break just like that—like the seams of the earth
suddenly ripped wide open, every great triumph and tribulation
bleeding onto the vacant streets we once wandered when we were
still kids, still giggling vessels of hope, still innocent enough to trust
the safety of the stitching, that promise of freedom unthreatened.

I love you so I let myself cry over the lack of you. Over the memory
of the place we once shared, when it was still as good as the day God
breathed it real, the rolling hills and the fog and the infinity of touch,
feel, taste. *Look around. It's ours and nothing can change that, not now,*

not yet, not ever.

Then We'll Be Happy We Made It

Maybe when the air cools, and it's mid-October and the farmers market stands are lined with jars of homemade apple butter, and the whole earth lurches forward in steady motion again, children cartwheeling and climbing and pleading for five more minutes in the dying sun, receiving the nod of approval and screeching *You're it!* to unfreeze their endless game of catch-me-if-you-can, and the movie theaters open their doors for fifteen-year-olds on clammy-handed first dates, when we can wipe hysterical, stitch-in-the-side tears from each other's faces, when the doctors can come home satisfied with "just another day on the job," when small eyes can peer out of small airplane windows, thousands of feet up in the blue, when we can stop trimming our shirts to fashion barriers to block the bad air, when we can finally relearn how good it is to touch, to tremble, to clutch each other so tightly we burst blood vessels in the passion of doing so, when it's safe enough to do all the things we swore we'd do when we were young enough to believe any of it could ever get taken away, when we finally do those things and let our bodies tread in the waters of sensation, when I have you and you have me, maybe it can just be October, just a good day.

Flickers of Promise

Meanwhile the world goes on—

and gap-toothed children still go about believing in
Santa Claus and closet monsters and imaginary friends.
The birds still sing their same tune from the treetops as
if they have no clue what sort of world we now live in, or
maybe they do and this is just their way of pretending not.
It would be so easy to give up on a dying world if not for
these flickers of promise: azalea bush outside my window
blooming in scarlet, drumbeat in my chest begging me to
Stay, stay, stay. It's springtime and I'm hollow but innocence
grows everywhere. Sprouts are rising from my garden pots and
soon it will be warm and I'll be next to you again. The wait will
be worth its while. In the meantime, people will be people and
I'll still be the writer, observer of this holy unraveling: stars that
choose to take their place in the heavens no matter who sticks
around to see them, or who doesn't, or who can't. This life does
not perform for anyone, not me, not you. It just is.
Meanwhile the world goes on—

and I stop to listen
to its quiet music,
infinitely looping.

Age of Innocence

Have you ever thirsted for a return to innocence?
Here is our land—iron red and tainted by illness,
pulpits occupied by witless politicians salivating
for power. Here is a twang at the heart—for anyone
small enough to be born into this vast unwelcome.

Perhaps I, too, have never known real innocence at all.
I was too young to remember how the world looked
before the planes struck the first tower. But I know it
happened. This land does not let you forget what pain
it felt. Maybe my age of innocence was never innocent
at all, but even still, it was much closer, universes more
tender. Here is what I remember—we thought of life

as charming. We didn't spend all day searching for hope,
tapping fortified plastic touchscreens to same-day ship
it to our front doors. We went to school without masks
on, never felt our hearts drop at the mere sight of a bulky
trench coat. Here is a portrait of the world I knew—

I was happy. It wasn't perfect but I was happy enough
to believe it could be, and that it would be forever, that
place where people smiled, and held open doors, where
we weren't forced to make thirteen-year-old girls clutch
pepper spray on the way home from middle school. How
I thirst for their innocence the way I had it. I could walk

without looking over my shoulder. Breathe without the possibility of quarantine. Love without fear that a law could somehow make it illegal, that sanctions could be made overnight, under cover of darkness, a body being stolen and thrown into the river to drown, unnoticed.

Poor Connection

Twenty-first century lovesickness: I am tired
of only holding you through a pixelated screen.

It's supposed to be good enough. But I yearn
for conversations under crabapple trees, chapped
lip kisses, a love that is less hope and more touch.

Does anyone even remember how anymore?

Sweat and spit and strands of hair.
Limbs unfolding. The delicious sweetness of longing
for something ripe and flaming and palpable.

I know you and I do. We've crammed a whole
lifetime of it in a handful of short,
sweltering months.

For now,

it's video calls until the early hours,
my heart begging to leap through the glass.

Good enough to pass the days. But Lord,

how I dream of those trees.

Something to Believe

It's me
and this tragic blank page,
and our next-door neighbor wielding
some sort of deafening machinery to tidy up
the rose bushes that appear to have devoured even
their front door, and a half-full mug of unsweetened
Japanese green tea that has since given up its heat for the sake
of my disappointing writing, and the feeling of *Damn, so much
of absolutely nothing has happened this year*, and the page filling up
with lifeless, lackluster poetry every night. It's me and this insatiable
loneliness, me and touch-starvation, me and these incurable bouts of
missing you until I fall asleep, if I even do. It's me and forgetting
the involuntary reaction to human touch, that elbow-to-elbow
peace of a city crowd, of being a buoy in a sea of hot breath,
so much closeness and so little air to separate it. I hate that
I can't write or see you or lose myself in the world. Or
that I'm running low on vital hoping. For now, it's
me and the hatred of this calendar year, and how
the neighbor has stopped loudly grinding away
at the stubborn weeds that needed tending
to because at least, when he was, that
gave me something to listen to,
something small to believe in
for at least a few minutes.

I Will Not Give up on You, America

because I have seen the cool blue of your mountains
and heard the voices of your children rising to meet them.

It almost feels like enough

until I let the soles of my feet sink sufficiently into your soil
and feel myself become an intruder of a deeper, untold story.

Sometimes I swear I can still hear the dead scream
just standing there, listening to your heartbeat—

red, white, blue—

The dead that built you. The dead you buried.

America, I want to believe in your goodness.

That you are still a breathing, wild thing,
that grace grows apart from your gardens and cities,
that there is more to you than just your wickedness.

Tell me the story.

Read to me so I can help you

rewrite it.

This World Isn't My Type Anymore

In my letters I write *Things have been good! As good as they can be these days!*, forced reassurance leaking through black ballpoint ink, unpoetic lines smeared by a heavy hand. What I mean by *good* is that I've got my hand stuck in a mixed bag. Some mornings I rise to an all-encompassing sense of dread, my body an anchor in a sea of boiling blood. Other mornings, though, I just make cinnamon oatmeal. Or a bagel with a thick layer of cream cheese. I'll put on the radio and lie in bed for an extra hour and not miss out on anything. At least I won't feel like I am. I've learned this life can feel sort of safe in the absence of the real thing. I'm not in love with it like I once was, no longer sucking the juice out of every short day I'm given, no longer chewing the rind for more. Content with what I can get—a hot shower, a vase of fresh flowers, an ounce of attention from the house cat—it's enough. I'm not rationing joy. I've just stopped chasing after it. I just let it chase me, let it serenade me, let it fall first.

There Were Good Things, Too

Like that one time my friends and I ordered a pepperoni pizza so grotesquely large it couldn't fit through the apartment door horizontally and how the slices were bigger than two of our heads stacked on top of each other. I have found that there are perks to the apocalypse and sometimes they look like greasy paper towels and football on TV featuring the eeriness of empty stadiums and lack of belligerent cheering that makes normal feel *normal*. We're accidental artists of making the most out of living, even when it's been seven months of isolation and bad news and unexpected obituaries, when all of California is on fire, when our streets are stained with blood, when *right* and *wrong* have blended together until the definitions eventually became horrifyingly interchangeable, when it feels as if the timeline itself has torn at its seams, spilling the guts of humanity onto the fabric of the universe and staining it, when it's another morning in a broken simulation and it's far too easy to believe in the cruelty of this world. I want to remember that there were good things, too. Like how we were all here together, feeling the weight of it all on a Friday evening, haunted by old dreams, how we collectively decided, *To hell with it all, why don't we just order a pizza?*

I'll Take That

Safe things—Mitski on my record player, my mother's thin fingers French-braiding my hair, bananas that are just ripe enough—I hold onto these safe things as I let my mind unravel in my hands. Today I feel a little bit better than yesterday. *I'll take that,* I tell the ceiling, as I remind my body to inhale without thinking too deeply about *how.* I'm tired of thinking about illness and death and why my chest hurts all the time. I'm sick of making myself sick. And so I clutch these harmless, healthy things with every gram of strength I have. Outside my house right now, someone is firing a gun. Every so often, my mother and I jump. But it's nothing, it's nothing, and she finishes the braid and we're humming, we're humming, and I'm still alive in a room that loves me, and no part of me is dead.

Today, After Too Many Consecutive Ones Spent Panicking

I did not panic.

Instead, I caught the bus without crying and texted my mom that I didn't.

Nor did I think much about death or check my pulse fifty times to make sure it hadn't found me yet.

Instead, I made myself a sunflower butter and blueberry jam sandwich and ate every bite of it on a park bench, crusts included, without letting the morsels of guilt get stuck in my teeth or in my throat.

I did not panic.

Today is the first day of September and you drove me to the drugstore in the rain to pick up my new prescriptions. On the way there we sang along to cheesy country songs written about the pandemic.

I did not think much about the pandemic.

Later, after binging *How I Met Your Mother* like we always do, we talked about the future over death-by-chocolate ice cream. A year from now who knows where we'll be.

I did not panic.

Instead, I held you close and told you I loved you

and did not think about how long I'd be able to—

I just did.

When My Kids Ask Me Why I Write

Well, I'll tell them,

sometimes you wake up and twist your ankle on the way downstairs
before a very important meeting, and later you find out it is shattered
in four different places, and even though you have big things to do
you must sit very still and wait for them to fuse again. Sometimes
you wake up and it's pouring rain so you make a pot of bold coffee
and read the news and it's just as depressing as yesterday's headlines
and so you decide to do something mindless like fold clean laundry
into categorized piles and then the phone rings and you find out
that someone you love has died, and so you stop folding clothes
and start shaking like a stilt house in a hurricane, and you forget
about the laundry and the coffee and the rain, and so you write.
Sometimes waiting isn't fair, I'll tell them. And sometimes
you must put the world on pause, turn off the television,
and let whatever is broken heal over, bones hardening until
you are whole enough to move. That's why I write, dear child,
because sometimes people die and the interstates are flooded
and another church was bombed in a city you can't pronounce
but you have a pen and a mind and a heart that can't stop bleeding.

Why do I write? Because what else would I do with all of this waiting?

I Talk to No One Else

Listless and unromantic, I wallow
to the skipping of rain on my roof.
Bedroom walls make alright lovers
when no one else is around to fill
these echoing caverns of silence.
I'm tired, I whisper to nothing,
and not in the way you think.
Tired like it's the wet season
in my hometown, and I miss
your baby hairs and peach fuzz
and the whole anatomy of you,
more *there* than my own skin.

There Will Be More

long walks home, more *Come on Eileen* on loop
blaring through sunroofs open wide, more plum
lipstick staining the Adam's apples of the boys
we love, more *you hang up first, I did last night,*
more sneaking one last kiss before the door shuts,
more cruising through the rich neighborhoods,
Christmas Eve, imagining their lofty electric bills
while Sinatra blankets the air as purely as the snow
we scarcely get around here, more pressing palms
together, finding where our heart lines intersect,
where our life lines end, more saving pictures of
dream dresses for our weddings still many years
away, more learning that sometimes the only real
prayer we have is blind hope, skeletons of faith,
clinging to the promise that *there will be more,
there has to be,* we have to get home somehow.

V

War Diary

Hibiscus

The mind is most honest when the stars are out.
There are no pretenses. There are no hideaways.
After midnight, I lie awake and dream of things
too shy for daytime. Things that go unspoken,
like how the pink hibiscus flowers on the shirt
he wore when he took what was not his, what
I never asked for, what I never gave him, those
flowers still bloom on the backs of my eyelids
when I try to sleep. Bloody petals, split stems,
no matter the season they are always there, like
weeds that return even after pulling, even after
all evidence has been erased, the roots devoured
by solid earth, they still grow without mercy.
The mind is most honest when the stars are out.
And I see him now, in the act of taking, cotton
and sweat, my voice begging him *no*, and hibiscus.

Facedown in the Grass

I am sick, Mom.

I am so sick that I convinced myself
I'd been reincarnated as a glass sculpture,
abstract and unmoving, against the pale blue
hydrangeas at the butterfly gardens today.

I am too sick for the gardens, Mom.

You took me there to forget myself, I know,
to feel—for a fleeting moment—less *hostage
of my mind* and more *dragonfly surfing
the lilypond.* But nothing ever becomes
of your worthy endeavors and I am fated
to be the dead among the living, the girl lying
facedown in the grass, praying for the grave.

Take me home, Mom.

I am sorry that I cannot grow,
that I am not a wild, blooming thing
capable of being swayed by summer air
and wanting nothing more than to live.
Mine are the roots that cannot clutch, Mom—
and maybe I am far too sick to stay.

I Said No

It's not about the act itself but the aftermath. After it happened I couldn't pass by a mirror for months without resurrecting the image of handprints on hips, the kind that didn't scrub off in the shower no matter how hard I tried, burning my bones, the memory of bruises reddening my ribs. I remember slinking back into my father's sweatshirt and leaving in the morning like nothing happened. You were fast asleep and I didn't wake you—just slipped on yesterday's wrinkled clothes, ran my hands through the knots in my hair you made when I was too dizzy to tell you to stop, and put last night's unfinished homework, stained amber by your cheap liquor, back into my school backpack, unfeeling. And then I didn't feel anything for the rest of the year. But after I left your dorm room that morning I got coffee. Two cups of half-and-half coffee creamer into a medium-sized styrofoam cup of dark roast. I took the window desk on the third floor of the library and wrote a mediocre essay on the Dark Lady in Shakespeare's Sonnet 130 through a post-structuralist lens. At the campus ice cream shop that night, over double scoops of mint chocolate chip in a waffle cone, a close girlfriend of mine asked me what was new in my world, and I said, *Nothing much, just looking forward to Thanksgiving break,* and adjusted the collar of my shirt so she wouldn't see what you did. That was the beginning of my fear of love. It's not about the act itself but the aftermath. The cavernous space between the me I knew and the me that couldn't be touched without the compulsion to scream. If anyone asked about you then I would've lied through my teeth and said something along the lines of *We're good. We're not together anymore but we're good.* I wouldn't have told them about the way you made me swallow a pill *just in case, I don't know, just do it*. I wouldn't have told them about crossing paths with you later that week, that all-knowing smirk plastered on your face, and how seriously I contemplated the height of a rooftop and whether or not it could eradicate my suffering. It's not about the act itself but the aftermath. It was the way I kept going, pretending we were still best friends, that the night never happened, that we just fell asleep and nothing more, and you took nothing.

Everyone has their own share of myths.

This is the one I've been telling. Until now.

Truce

Staredown between the neon orange bottle
and my hand already cupped in anticipation.

This unfolding drama is what I do not tell you.
The story goes like this: *I almost do and then*

I don't. Count to ten. Thing of the good things,
like mother taught you when you were young

and yet sad enough to die. I've been rehearsing
the good things for decades. Orange marmalade

and rich people's lawns that water themselves,
my records from the '70s and the sepia freckles

that scatter across the nose of the man I love.
I'll stay for that, I guess, and the staredown ends.

September, in My Head

will always bring back visions of my body, nearly nineteen,
crumpled like an old shirt in the corner of a dorm room
belonging to a boy I thought loved me. Poor girl, if only
I could scoop her up from the cold tile and feed her bowls
of her mother's homemade chicken noodle soup, if I could
finger the coarse knots from her unwashed hair, if I could
tell her to run from anyone who tries to claim her skin
as their own. September, in my head, is a kind of winter
nothing ever prepares me for, no matter how many pass
before my eyes. Every September, I am eighteen again,
and I'm waiting for him to stop laughing at how small
I feel, weeping hard into purple knees and wondering
what else I must give up to deserve a kiss goodnight.

When I Try to Imagine the Woman for Whom You'd Leave Me

there are no pills in sight, no crumpled just-in-case goodbye letters,
no clumps of hair on her desk from far too much worrying for you.

Her friends (she has them) would describe her as *bubbly* or *bright,*
certainly not *difficult* or *temperamental* (it's fine; I've made peace).

She can design a mean bouquet. She has a signature dish. She could
even be a model, though her humility prevents this. She has the frame

for it. If she writes poetry (though unlikely) she'd never write a poem
titled "When I try to imagine the woman for whom you'd leave me."

She sticks to nature. Childhood. The simplicity of her love for you.
She's a damn good writer and she doesn't need an ounce of trauma

to write things you'd read. In my head, I see green eyes and fair skin
and confidence that never borders on cocky. But I do not see sadness.

I do not see the variety that my body, awkward and uncouth, emits.
I could recognize it anywhere. But not in her, your Aphrodite, holy

human cathedral. She talks about the past. She has no mean streak.
Even I would pray to her. I would consecrate myself at her shrine

for having everything I cannot call my own. When I try to imagine
the woman for whom you'd leave me I see someone even I would

accidentally love. Her easy poetry and femininity and lack of grief.
Her way with flowers and food and loving you without killing you.

Someone Better

Mom,

One day I'll be happy enough
to not cry on your birthday.
I won't have to beat my fists against
the slope of my skull
or purple my thighs over the unfair ordeal
of having a brain like mine. I wish
I could be an easy daughter, that I could
find you a better one on the highest shelf
of a seaside gift shop and swaddle her
in wrapping paper to place in your hands,

someone better

who won't hate the body you gave her
the kind of someone you deserve

but never got.

A Little Less Fire

A privilege it would be
to be a little less fire.

Less microcosm of chaos. Less coming apart at the seams.
Less doubled-over Holy Lance, millennia still bleeding.
Less scarlet fever soul. less gunfire.
Less gaping mouth, letter O, still sounding.

To be, instead,
more pastoral meadow. More cherub on cathedral ceiling.
More first real love, years still sweet, still sore.
More sleeping baby. More sky before snow.
More mother's touch. More Sunday morning, still quiet.

The definition of Paradise is this
and it is lost to me.

I fear I have fallen from the grace of myself.

Without Your Name, Who Are You?

I still don't know. I wish I had words for this strange curse:
the way I accidentally leave hearts gasping for oxygen
like pathetic fish out of water, how I cannot move
even an inch without burning someone, or something.
I am comprised of far too much intensity. If my body had
a list of ingredients, it would read *fire, inferno, conflagration,*
the label burned at the edges, the fine print charred black as night.

How strange—I'm a water sign. Yet so much of me incinerates.
Fire is familiar. Fire is home to me. I am safe among embers.

This I know because my poetry bleeds like a glass of wine
plummeting into the lap of a white dress. And my heart, too,
bleeds like a sunset spilling into the ocean: no boundaries,
no laws enforced or governed, an open wound I can't stop picking at.

I am both the abandonment and the abandoned,
both the water and the fish, both the sea of flames
and the body at the stake, burning, burning, then burned.

And I'll love you just like that, too, scarlet tragedy.
A pretty, giggling, mesmerizing nightmare,
writing you into poetry that melts holes in your hands.

Eighteen Years

My eighteenth birthday was spent crying on the shore of a frozen beach.
It was all I requested: poetry books and a weekend with the ocean.
My parents and I wore parkas in mid-November,
the frigid breath of late autumn blowing wet sand into our faces.
That night, I bundled up on the balcony, drunk on sparkling cider
and the tragedy of being me.
The loneliness of finally being old enough
to understand that the ocean cannot cure every sickness.
That only time can heal open wounds, and that
saltwater can only do so much to stop the infection.
Sand cannot quell the bite of heartache,
the nostalgic pang of birthdays past–
a time of candles, dripping wax,
and when blowing them out
(Happy birthday to you,
happy birthday to you,
happy birthday dear–)
didn't feel so hollow.

I have forgotten what I wished for.
Maybe a sailboat, maybe a car ride home,
maybe a sunrise that didn't sting.

I Don't Know What You're Scared Of

but for me, it's formal dining rooms and how to eat neatly in them
and family portraits with everyone clad in the same shade of beige
and how unlike your mom is from my mom and how unlike you
are from me, even though I hunger for you and would like to sit
with you in the car with your brothers while you talk about what
I don't understand, like football and Catholic school and loving
your hometown even after leaving it. I want to tell you the reason
why these things scare me but I'm too invested in the pearliness
of your skin, yet another region of unlikeness, and the strange way
I touch you and feel ivory and snowfall and Jesus and America
and everything I wanted to be when I was younger and obsessed
with purity, whiteness, the privilege I could taste on my first love's
lips, later stuck in my teeth, then in my throat. I'm not scared
of you, not at all, but the way I choke back my first language
when I shake hands with the world that will never welcome it.

Sometimes I Hate Poetry

because it feels like pulling invisible threads
through clogged pores or dry heaving foreign
objects of nothingness lodged somewhere
between the throat and chest cavity. I hate
poetry occasionally for the way it leaves my
ego wrung dry and desperate and my frame
brittle and these red eyes glazed over entirely
as if they have seen too much to hold any of it.
There are days when excavating the mind for
the most worthy words feels like an errand left
to run or another heart left to break reluctantly
and be done with forever, killing something real.

*I'd like to write about flowers tonight or how
we witnessed the first real sunset all winter
through the blinds of your apartment kitchen
or how I hate everything about the past few years
except meeting you and loving you and keeping
you. Or maybe something about how I miss home
but don't at the same time because everything there
reminds me of everything I've lost and being there
makes me pray I could give up my history, but I can't,
because doing so would mean killing something real.*

Nights like tonight everything I write feels pitiful,

like crying at the dentist or not knowing what to say when someone new asks me where I'm from. I hate poetry some days because no matter how hard I try to pull those invisible threads through my skin once and for all, I lose grip. They slip back in, pointless to the point of no return, objects of nothingness.

Patron Saint of Trying

On bad days I like to pretend the universe knows me.

That she's memorized the way I pick at my split ends, how my left eye's only lazy in photos, how I grew up dreaming of one day becoming the patron saint of something wild. Like bad poetry or bipolar disorder or far too much passion to fit inside a five-foot-five frame. Imagine that—being martyred for a cause worth dying for. Even now I'd still die for emotion.

I fantasize over the stars knowing the things I hold secret to my soul, of the moon looking back at me in complete understanding. All of these celestial bodies daring to acknowledge my own, choosing to find the horror film starlet crying on the floor of the shower, mourning the loss of belief. I am no saint. I like to imagine the universe seeing this— that she could recognize the expression on my face.

I like to pretend she's been observing me for twenty years. That she saw the flicker in my eye when I was born and knew that I'd be the patron saint of trying.

Holy fantasies, how you consume me. The cosmos could not be more indifferent, yet the dream rages on.

These Days

I tell people *I grew tired of feeling,*
so I decided to stop. Just like that.
Cut the melodrama. I have matters
to tend to. Weeds to pull, papers
to write. No capacity for mourning,
no time to process, no mental space
for any kind of earth-shattering emotion.
I'd like to order a blank slate, please,
I bargained with the universe one night,
so apparently, this is just how I live now.
I just wake up each day and promise
to keep composure. I control the flux.
I am my own government.

A new law: nothing can seep into my skin
if I don't touch it. It's that simple.

But it's impossible for me to move
and not be moved. This I realized
as I watched probably the thousandth
sunset of my life bleed into the horizon
and felt its colors seeping into me, too.

VI

Swan Songs

I Am Writing to Tell You

That I have learned to accept that good things exist

although I know that in your head I am a cynic
cursing our old friends and letting go of the wheel
forcing fate to pick what comes next. And I know
that *whiplash* and *fury* are the images of me you've kept
and that you remember the ease of which I drained
bottles and bawled the torment out of my lungs
from the balcony and how they almost called the cops
before you took me back to your place and rocked
me to sleep because I couldn't do it on my own

but I am writing to tell you

that I haven't screamed in months and instead
I write poems about August and paint landscapes
of the Rockies although I've never been and now
I take my medicine and pour my life into letters
that I send across the country and I only think
about you when it rains and never out of spite

I am writing to tell you

that I am getting a dog soon and last week I cut my hair
like I do when someone breaks my heart except this time

no one did, I think I just like change now

which I know is foreign to you because back then
you watched me give myself bruises when he decided
he couldn't handle my anger and made me walk home
alone and how afterwards I made you burn my journals
because I couldn't stand seeing that life on paper

I don't want to die anymore

and I don't think you ever met this version of me

in the three years I've loved you and I wonder

if you are still the most tender person in the universe
like I remember you, holding my hair back
from sinking into the toilet water and weeping
with me when I'd talk about the frozen river
under the bridge and how I wanted to marry it

I am writing to tell you

that right now I am eating leftover Chinese food
because I don't hate the way I look in pictures anymore
and that yesterday I spun around in the satin slip I wore
the night of my birthday when you called me a goddess
and how I punched you in the stomach, my little liar,
I wanted to hate you for making me love myself

but I am writing to tell you

that I do now.

I grip the wheel.

I am good to my body.

I want to live.

If Eve Were Not of Eden

I imagine she'd *talk back bleach her hair cry to records that skip.*
Would she *wear ripped jeans love the wrong boy ruin the right one?*
If Eve didn't earn her fame for plucking forbidden fruit I imagine
she'd be wicked good company. She'd be all *60 in a 45 windows
down blasting the profane music.* Eve would *giggle at all the sick jokes
read all the censored books do it all without batting an eyelash.*
If Eve were not of Adam would we care for her at all?
If she were less stolen rib and more *flammable woman?*
If Eve were not the doer of damnation, the action cursed,
the forever receiver of our shaking fists, I imagine
I might adore her, *to be brave enough to risk perfection
for freedom, to be bigger than the garden,
than even knowledge, to be bold enough
to reach and pull.*

Mortal Stardust

after Joni Mitchell's "Woodstock"

Bathed in sunlight, I feel almost human.
Must be the antidote to my strangeness,
spine melting into wet soil, facing the ether.
How strange it is to inhabit a body, mortal
stardust, cosmic temple. Nothing earthly
has ever eased me. But there is a feeling like
coming home or *holiness* or *divinity* when
my bones are clothed by warmth. To feel
seen by the sky, pursued by its glow, how
it overcomes me. *Remember that you are
stardust and to stardust you shall return.*
The infinite calls me Child. Endlessness
breathes my name and I listen, obedient.

Life Moves Above Awareness

I am thinking of the things we leave behind before we even have the chance to notice. Skin cells and soulmates and stories. Strands of loose hair in the shower, fingerprints on escalator handrails, shot glances, minor details of our histories *(what you ate for breakfast on your first day of sixth grade)*, these small things of which we do not care enough to store for safekeeping. Life moves above awareness and permanence is only as permanent as it feels. This I know because there came a day I found myself standing very still in the middle of a bustling sidewalk stranded in a city, a moment, a life I could not recognize. The natural question came to mind: *How did I get here?* as I stood in a body unknown to me, alien vessel drowning in a sea of colors I could not name. Sensory overload, system failure, panic. Cars drove past without noticing, time still set in motion with no regard for who chooses to stand motionless. It hit me then and there, in the eye of my own hurricane, that everything I shed—hair ties left behind on ex-boyfriends' nightstands, poems written on the backs of coffee shop napkins crumpled and tossed into train station garbage cans, an old phone number saved in a dead friend's phone—took me here. It was all my doing. Every act unnoticed is still an act after all.

Praise to the Holy Habitual

The story goes like this.

One day you're sitting in a living room on a Friday night with the family you chose for yourself, howling laughter ricocheting off apartment walls, everyone seeing double. We're fifteen bodies content in perfect company, pushing the limits of a noise complaint from the neighbors, but singing out anyway, because *we are here, we are here*

and then we're not

and we may never be again

at least not in the same way.

Perfect configurations, these habitual moments
we hold close but never quite close enough.

For a brief moment in time we were just twenty-somethings kicking our shoes off by the door to stay for a while.

That's the story.

It has no ending

but maybe that's what makes it worth telling.

We were there,
we were there,
we were there.

I could sing it out forever.

Tunnel Vision

When the movie of my life plays before my eyes, a recap of however many years I've collected, when I'm clinging onto the skin of it by a thinning thread and the faint music hums in that near-death glimmer of a blinding light, I wonder what I'll see. The other night I wept over the idea, living tears burning my body, one day gone, this temporary vessel. What will be my final vision, passing from this world to whatever cryptic life (or lack thereof) exists apart from this one? Who will be waiting for me at the finish line, holding a poster? What will it say?

I've been too many people for too many people. I've played hero and villain and wounded thing crouching in the corner of a bad man's bedroom. I've played the other woman and your only woman and the shivering woman, dipping her toe into the frigid waters of an unknown river, half-alive and tempted to drown.

Maybe, in that long-awaited slideshow of memory, I'll greet every great love of my life again, every pair of eyes I've adored, lingering for a brief moment just to warm myself by those familiar fires. I'm a lucky one. I've been seen by so many.

I'll watch myself break and bloom all over again. There's no use crying now.

When I reach God, in all of his unfathomable might, he'll smile and ask me, "How did you like your life?" and I'll look down and whisper, "Which one?"

I Like It Here

Where sheep graze lazily
around the sunset-stained silo across our street.
I live in a world fit for a stamped postcard,
wild purple berries lining the valley paths
and tree-covered hideaways, where stillness
is not only allowed but encouraged.
Nothing is demanded of the farmland wanderer,
perfumed by morning dew and inebriated
by the gentleness of a dying August.
I like it here, where the wild river twists
in its rugged beauty, where the sky breaks
open enough for me to hear my heartbeat
singing *I am alive, I am alive,*
I know I am alive.

Portrait of Eve

after Jorie Graham, Sylvia Plath

I understand you now. The gesture, too.
You just wanted something to sink your teeth into.

And so you plucked. The bough frowned.
So did God. And Adam, still unseeing, felt something in him crumple.

The fabric of the universe wrinkled. The veil of time tore in two.
Before and after. Before you plucked, after you tasted.

How sweet this song of womankind.
Eternity bores me,
I never wanted it.

Skin torn, letting the juice drip to the elbows.
How apple-crisp is rebellion, that chewing and swallowing of freedom?

I get it, beautiful sister of mine.
You had your eye on it from the moment it began growing.
It's what we do best, giving nothing up.

But giving,
for eternity, in.

Quietudes

for my childhood neighborhood

Bathed in blushing light, I do not dwell
upon death for the first time in weeks.
Instead, I let the atoms of my body
make cosmic love to sidewalk shadows,
a strange sensation of fulfillment soaring
past the treetops of this miniature world.
I welcome it—these rare quietudes—
where I can lay my armor down
and think of nothing else beyond
the forgiveness of sun
on living skin.

Citizens of Beauty

I pledge allegiance
to Octobers in the Blue Ridge,
her autumn air a sincere sort of baptism.
And to the weeping branches of the willow trees
where I sit at the pond and weep over everything
I have given away, leaves fluttering as if they can listen,
as if they are. To the grazing cows, to the noisy streams,
to the orchid skies we melt beneath, our spines engraving
into damp earth, both of us high on petrichor. It is grace
to be a citizen of beauty. To be sons and daughters of
valleys where wildflowers spring in the snow, to be
the dumb and baffled children swept in her seas.
To the fields striped with yellow and the mossy
troves, to the kisses we exchange under paling
moonlight, to the stars that keep our prayers,
I pledge allegiance to you and you alone.

Names and Trees and Variations of God

I like to go for walks around the manmade pond near my apartment complex and take low-quality pictures of the massive weeping willow that looms over the asphalt bike path. I do this solely for the purpose of curating evidence in my camera roll that I am, in fact, still alive. Sometimes I forget. I think that, in a world like ours, forgetting is becoming more and more acceptable. It feels good to forget. Think about it. There eventually comes a day when someone casually brings up a name in conversation—*that* name, you know which one I'm talking about—the name you swore you'd never be able to hear without feeling your insides weaken into gelatin, body crumpling into nothing but blood and guts—and then you realize that the name—*that* name—hasn't crossed your mind all morning for the first time in a handful of hellish months. Forgetting feels a little like religion. Like hearing whoever God is to you, speaking within the innermost chamber of your heart. Forgetting can make you want to write a sappy love letter to the universe: *thank you for setting me free!* Sometimes I forget I am a person who will one day, like every other person who has ever been and will ever be, die. So I go for walks with headphones on, blasting the music of my parents' generation. Sometimes no music at all, just me in my infinite silence, taking photos of the foliage to save for later. These days I like to save some things for myself. I like to remember. I like hearing my name.

Barefoot Into the Deep

The ocean is a healing rage. Medicinal fury, restorative wrath. I feel connected to the water, knowing it has mingled with the branches of my ancestry. We all wade in the same recycled substance, every life connected by what falls from the heavens. Water is a cyclical being, prone to temper tantrums, almost too easily offended. I, too, am turbulent. I live forever misunderstood. Maybe this is why, running haphazardly and barefoot into the deep, I am overcome by the knowledge that I am fully known in this moment, where I do not have to pretend I am anything but a buoyant body, calm at long last. The ocean understands. We speak the same mother tongue, back and forth in crashing waves, tender darkness.

Do Not Let Me Run

so fast I forget to absorb the *now now now* of being where my feet are. I refuse to reduce these years to blurred half-truths and half-asleep rainy mornings I spend on the nauseating bus humming down Prices Fork Road. I want to remember the stickiness of the rain here, even in the bitter cold mud of the New River Valley where everything ironically feels old, nothing *new* at all, the very soil we stand on worked by human hands deeper than anywhere I've ever been rooted. Do not let me forget the electricity of this place. How holy the fog on a Sunday morning, how charged the stars every night I stumble home in the dizzy glory of a twenty-something dreamer. Do not let me call these open fields anything but home, these cornfield paths, the jagged and unexpected trails left behind by speeding bicycles cutting through the farmland, the sheer audacity of the springtime to be this tender on the soul, and the silent horses stopping to observe us as we pass, thinking of nothing but the kindness of our company.

Visions of a Life

That feeling—a nighttime walk in the crepuscular light
of late November, leaves crunching under rain boots
I wore by accident, having misunderstood the forecast
while rushing to catch the late bus in the morning.

There's a certain kind of magic in *that kind* of being alone,
wandering home at half past seven, taking the longer route
just to bask in the breeze for a moment more. It's hard not
to peer through the golden windows of other people's
homes without appearing freakish and unnatural. But I do

anyway, sometimes, as they fold their laundry or put away
dinner plates or chat with their mothers on the phone.
Sometimes I'm lucky enough to catch a warm embrace
shared under the kitchen light fixtures. Sometimes I don't
catch anything at all, just a dim room and a cat perched
on the ledge. A messy desk. An unwatered houseplant.

There's a fondness in feeling momentarily at home in the world.

Periphery

When I blur away the countryside, sixty-five miles per hour shuttling through the Shenandoah Valley, everything feels right again. There's something potent about living on the fringes of things. From the backseat window, I reduce the world to color—lines of dairy cows merely black and white brushstrokes decorating a living green canvas, all scenery rushing before my eyes converted to watercolor. It's much safer to inhabit a place like this. No one has anything to say, nothing to purge nor wield. In this place no language is necessary, for there is no real life here, only pigments colliding with loose shapes, edges bending and lacking, my own dizzy mayhem. How I adore this incomprehensible movement. Here the world spills into itself. No one stops it from doing so. Today I'm heading home and it feels right. I've got The Four Seasons' "Can't Take My Eyes Off You" melting my brain to candle wax, daydreams as pliable as modeling clay, and cumulus clouds hanging above me as unapologetic as ever, specially designed for getting lost in.

Today I Am Not an Open Wound

but a poem.

Something blooming, all peony pink
and fresh-petaled, swaying in the sweetness of it all.
I am bubbles rising from soapy wands, less April shower
and more April *symphony:* what a way to blossom this is,
this springing (not falling) in love again,
this simple joy of praying to be picked.

Today I am not an open wound

but I used to be.

And I thank these clear skies for that ancient history of mine.
For crumpling on bathroom floors and breaking in stalls,
for yellow, tender bruises, for the wrong love.
I say thank you to the torrential downpour
of *too much girl, never enough reasons to stay.*

Today I'll put on a record, a love letter to the universe.
It's broken. It skips. I play it anyway. I even sing.

thank you, thank you, thank you—

for taking from me what I thought
I could not live without

thank you, thank you, thank you—

for more space to dance.

I Will Not Go Gentle

after Dylan Thomas

I will not go gentle

into any good night. This body
loves its rage. I will not sit back
for any show. When it comes time
to depart I will do it with a throat
sore from screaming. Bruised knees
and fingertips charred from toying
with embers. I will not submit
to the silence of slipping away.
I will leave with bloodshot eyes
and shattered bones. Skin torn
from having lived a life of feeling.
I will not leave before letting
the whole world know *I was here.*
I was here. I was here and to be me
was to make sure of it. I will not
leave under cover of darkness.
I will leave an echo. A porch light.
A poem. I will leave my love on.

GRATITUDE

I'd like to thank the following people for their instrumental support throughout my writing journey:

Mom, for being the first person to read every draft—from my preschool days to the final version of this book. You are my nonjudgmental confidante and my safe place to land.

Dad, for believing in me enough to challenge me, which requires more bravery and toughness than most people have. Out of everyone on this planet, I am convinced that I am most like you.

Andrew, to whom my volumes of love poems are dedicated. It is an honor to be your life companion and to weather the world in your presence.

Lola, for the privilege of being your "perfect princess." Life is not the same without your singing. I miss you every day.

Family, by blood and by choice, but especially my cousins, who make me forget I was ever born an only child.

Teachers and mentors in Woodbridge who held my hand long enough to eventually let go with confidence. You raised me into the writer I am today, and for that I am eternally grateful.

Professors, advisors, and the entire arts community at Virginia Tech, for instantly becoming my second home. This book would not exist without you.

Friends, and that I have them in abundance—for keeping me laughing and authentically myself.

Prince William County, Manassas, Manassas Park, the Arts Council, and the Poet Laureate Circle for choosing me to represent our corner of the world for the next two years.

Readers of both editions of *Cul-de-sac Angels*, for making it matter.

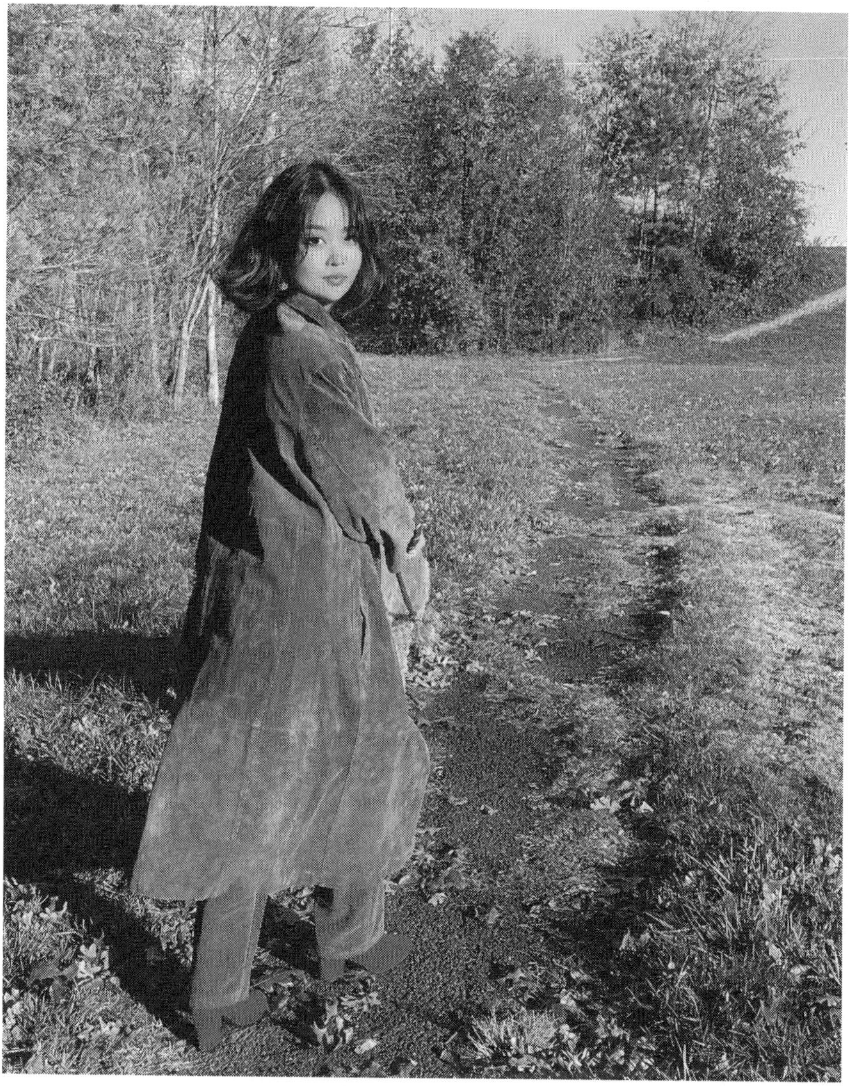

Michelle Garcia

is a 23-year-old Filipino-American poet, memoirist, and multimedia artist from Lake Ridge, Virginia. In 2022, she was crowned poet laureate of Prince William County, Manassas, and Manassas Park, Virginia, representing the Washington D.C. metropolitan area as an arts advocate, educator, and public speaker. Michelle is a Virginia Tech alumna, graduating summa cum laude in 2021 with degrees in English literature and language, creative writing, and communication science and social inquiry. Her writing has been published in *Philologia*, *Mim Magazine*, *Tenderheart Collective*, *PW Perspective*, *The Old Bridge Observer*, *Silhouette Literary and Art Magazine*, and other publications. The first edition of *Cul-de-sac Angels* was released in 2021 and instantly became an Amazon bestseller in women's poetry. Visit www.michellegarciawrites.com for more.